CHILD NEGLECT

UNDERSTANDING AND REACHING THE PARENT

A Guide for Child Welfare Workers

Norman A. Polansky
Christine DeSaix
Shlomo A. Sharlin

Child Welfare League of America, Inc.
67 Irving Place, New York, N.Y. 10003

4th printing 1976

Foreword

This book was written especially for social workers who, despite feeling overwhelmed by the knowledge required, are confronted with the most difficult of all casework responsibilities — helping the grossly neglectful parent and salvaging his child. It is thus useful across all fields and agencies where those two tasks exist, but such situations are found most extensively in the public social agencies of the country. Throughout the text the authors address themselves, therefore, to the public agency caseworker. The case material comes from public agency caseloads in North Carolina and Georgia, where the authors have been studying child neglect for some years. Their teachings are, of course, applicable everywhere, because children are everywhere being destroyed by neglect.

The present-day statutory structuring of public agencies to provide social services to families and to take on protective service functions emphasizes the book's timeliness, and the importance of the problem to both families and caseworkers makes me wish that this guide would find its way to every worker's desk. Its illumination of casework theory fuses perfectly — in magnificently jargon-free English — with the realities of practical experience, to yield a unique learning and teaching instrument. It is with great pleasure that the Child Welfare League of America makes it available to social work in general and the child welfare field in particular.

Carl Schoenberg
Director of Publications
Child Welfare League of America, Inc.

Preface

This book is an outcome of research in the rural mountains of western North Carolina and north Georgia. Initial scouting for the research began in 1964. Numerous lay and professional people who are involved with children focused on the neglected child as their greatest concern in child welfare. Many families were so overwhelmed by their own life problems they had given up trying to do more than the minimum for their children, and had abandoned themselves to apathy. From those charged with helping them, there was the recurrent query: "What does one do with such a family?"

Titled "The Apathy-Futility Syndrome in Child Neglect," a program of studies was supported through grants to the School of Social Work at the University of Georgia. As the title suggests, we were at work on two entwined problems: child neglect, and personalities prevalent among neglectful mothers. Our studies have taught us much, and in this book we try to transmit the gist of what we learned, in a form most usable in practice.

It is pleasant to acknowledge the contributions of others. We want especially to thank Mrs. Katherine R. Williams of our faculty, who participated actively in planning, pretesting and earlier phases of the writing. Her direct knowledge of the conditions of (rural) public agency work, combined with sophisticated training and experience, was invaluable. Donald R. Boone helped with critiques of the manuscript and contributed many ideas; Robert D. Borgman, Betty Jane Smith and Mary Lou Wing, former full-time staff members, each left an imprint on our thinking; Dean Charles Stewart of our school has taken a consistently thoughtful and supportive interest.

The research was supported by Program Grant SRS-89-P-800-55/4-01 (formerly PR-1200-2) from the Child Welfare Research and Demonstration Grants Program, Community Services Administration, Social and Rehabilitation Services, Department of Health, Education and Welfare. We are grateful to our grant manager, Mrs. Virginia K. White, for her help in arranging dissemination and advice about its content.

More than most, this book has undergone "visions and revisions," and has been tested out with two groups of workers in Georgia and North Carolina; we are indebted to them for reviewing preliminary drafts. Since none of these friends is to be held responsible for what follows, we credit them only with what is good.

Contents

CHAPTER ONE

The Problem

Historical Perspective

Intensive efforts to deal with child neglect have a surprisingly short history in this country. The early colonists had mixed feelings toward the economically dependent. Under the Judeo-Christian tradition they felt an obligation to help, but this was accompanied by a strong wish to spare the costs. If parents died or were rendered "impotent" (i.e., disabled) neighbors or the church might assume custody of the child with the understanding that he was to earn his keep and be reared to a "calling." Often, a poor orphan would be brought up at town meeting, to be auctioned to the lowest bidder—whoever would care for him at the least expense to the town treasury. Of course, this put a premium on getting the most work for the least food out of the youngster. Children were chattels, legally the property of their parents. Most will recall that Huckleberry Finn, of whom Mark Twain wrote in the mid-19th century, was an abused child in flight from his father and without legal protection.

A large children's agency was formed as late as 1853, and one of its stated intents was to rescue the respectable burghers of New York from the depredations of hungry, roving children of the streets. Compassion for stray cats and dogs and overworked dray horses led animal lovers to form the American Humane Association in 1866, but not until 1875 did they add a division devoted to the protection of mistreated children. We were into the present century before the battle to eliminate child labor was waged in earnest; the Constitution was interpreted as forbidding such legislation. This was a problem made worse by the industrial revolution. Sarah Cleghorn offers the piquant lines:[1]

The golf links lie so near the mill

That almost every day

1

The laboring children can look out
And see the men at play.

We were in the era of the New Deal before child labor laws became truly effective, and it was also during the 1930s that public concern for the standard of living of all our children became embedded in our legal structure, as one aspect of the social security legislation. With all the reservations that have grown up about the program, one has only to consider what went before—or what did not go on before—to appreciate Aid to Families of Dependent Children. By providing basic financial assistance, this program is one mainstay against gross child neglect.

By now, AFDC is an enormous system and, for some years, about 4% of our children have been covered by it at any one time. As of February 1970, for example, there were nearly 5½ million (5,482,698, to be exact) children on AFDC along with nearly 2 million adults for a monthly cost of over $350 million. For the fiscal year ending June 30, 1970, the cost of AFDC was $4,963,258,000. Beyond the elemental financial aid are all the so-called child welfare services, dedicated to meeting such problems as blindness, deafness, retardation, emotional disturbance—and neglect and abuse. As of March 31, 1969, there were 700,000 children under care of public agencies and another 250,000 being aided by private (i.e., nongovernmental) social organizations. A quarter of a million youngsters were in foster care at that time, and 74,000 were in institutions for the dependent, neglected and emotionally disturbed.[2]

We see, then, that although compassion for helpless children is a basic element of the ethical traditions on which this country was founded, it has taken almost two centuries for it to find widespread public expression in the programs we know so well. Millions of orphaned children, or those whose fathers are disabled, are protected by social security; millions of others, as we have noted, are buffered against the worst kind of want by AFDC.

Abuse or Neglect?

It has been customary in keeping agency statistics to lump together neglect, abuse and exploitation. But these are not by any means identical conditions, and more recently the experts have been treating them separately. There is good reason to believe the personalities of the parents involved are quite different. And, of course, the long-term effects on the victims are also markedly varied.

Child abuse has been defined by Gil as, "An occurrence in which a caretaker, usually an adult, injures a child, not by accident, but deliberately. ... Accordingly, the definition includes not only injuries due to acts of deliberate commission, but also acts of deliberate omission, such as malnutrition resulting from intentional withholding of food."[3]

The Problem

Following a series of nationally advertised incidents about the mid-1960s, public concern about child abuse has finally been translated into somewhat more effective legislation than we used to have, especially with respect to reporting suspected cases of child abuse. In a number of states, it is now mandatory that a person having reasonable cause to suspect abuse report it to the police or welfare department. An important advance is the protection against being sued for slander, which is now extended to the doctor, teacher or other citizen who reports. The presumption in these states is that such reports are generally made "in good faith" and "without malice."

The age of the victim of abuse is a factor in its incidence. It is reported most often among children aged 3 to 6, next most often among infants under 1 year of age. Child abuse seems to drop sharply when the child becomes old enough to run away. More boys than girls are reported abused. Pediatricians have been active in identifying abuse among very young children through the "battered child syndrome." An abused infant may show many old healed fractures in limbs and skull on X-ray examination. As we shall see, the identification and proof of child neglect demand quite different criteria.

In a classic study, Leontine Young found some marked differences between neglectful and abusing families. The two do not generally go together. Only a small proportion of neglected children are also abused. Whereas abusive parents typically restrict the child's social experience outside the home, neglectful parents do not actively forbid such attachments. Nor is the neglectful parent so prone to derogatory remarks about his child.

Most experts agree with Irving Kaufman, who maintained that "the (abusing) parents have a special kind of unhealthy interaction with the child—that is, the child has a special pathological meaning to the parents, or the parents use the child to act out their conflicts."[4] It is common to discover that the abusing parent was himself subjected to abuse or harsh punishment in his own youth. Not only does he have a reservoir of anger, but he strikes out at his child as if he has fused the child unconsciously with his own hated parents. On the other hand, as we shall see, the personality problems of neglectful mothers are likely to be more diffuse.

There seems to be little relationship between poverty and the need to attack a child. We know children who are well-fed, well-dressed, well-housed and yet treated cruelly. It is as if the parent wants to preserve the target of his venom. We have seen other children who undergo cold and malnutrition and periodic abandonment, but have never been struck or even physically punished by a parent.

In child abuse it often seems as if no one has had either the courage or the caring to intervene for the child. It is rather common for the nonabusing parent to collaborate in concealing the true state of affairs from the authorities, giving fear of retaliation as the reason.

3

Discovery of an abused child arouses anger, nausea and a desire to rescue the child in the general public. There are headlines and followup stories in the news media. And well there might be, for a case of child abuse uncovered usually represents not a single incident, but a recurrent pattern of torture by the parents. But without wishing to minimize the tragedy of abuse or the urgency of saving its young victims, neglect and its companion, marginal child care, affect many more children even though neglected children, for the most part, suffer silently in their own homes, unremarked by the world outside.

It is hard to get precise figures about child welfare services because states differ in their methods of reporting and some do not report centrally at all. We do have some pertinent data from North Carolina, which offered services to about 20,000 children in a typical recent year. In the year ending June 30, 1970, after all complaints had been investigated, 2,258 children were thought to be neglected. In the same year, 195 children were reported abused—a ratio of less than 10 to 1.[5]

Defining Neglect

When is there neglect? To a large extent, neglect is in the eye of the beholder. It is no wonder, therefore, that some complaints about it do not lead to a legal decision that it is present. On the other hand, there undoubtedly are many more situations that ought to be investigated but that are never reported. One reason, of course, is fear of retaliation by the accused parent. In the area of our research, where nearly all rural people are armed to a degree, neighbors and even relatives are chary of "getting involved." And the American Humane Association estimates that less than 10% of cases coming to the attention of agencies are ever brought to court.

There is another reason that no issue is made of the lives some children lead. The fact that "everybody in that hollow lives that way" does not make it all right, but the tendency is to dismiss whole groups of low-income people or those of nonwhite background as if they were not quite human.

At any rate, there is no established yardstick for measuring the point at which child care has sunk so low as to be called "neglect." Nor can we turn to the courts for decisions based on consistent precedents from which a criterion might be derived. Taking testimony from both lay and professional witnesses, each judge interprets the law as his wisdom and personal experience dictate.

A number of states, however, have attempted to deal with this by spelling out guidelines for protective service workers and the courts. In general, these embrace criteria laid down by the Children's Division of the American Humane Association:[6]

It is presumed that physical, emotional and intellectual growth and welfare are being jeoparidized when, for example, the child is

1. malnourished, ill clad, dirty, without proper shelter or sleeping arrangements;
2. without supervision, unattended;
3. ill and lacking essential medical care;
4. denied normal experiences that produce feelings of being loved, wanted, secure and worthy (emotional neglect);
5. failing to attend school regularly;
6. exploited, overworked;
7. emotionally disturbed due to constant friction in the home, marital discord, mentally ill parents;
8. exposed to unwholesome and demoralizing circumstances.

This is a legalistic definition. It sets down broad guidelines within which someone must still decide the specifics. When a young mother impulsively goes off and leaves her children unattended for several days, there is no problem. But, fortunately or unfortunately, the majority of cases that concern us are not so clearcut.

Identifying Neglect

There is a number of reasons why legislators have been unable to come up with a simple definition of child neglect. To begin with, there is the question of whom to look at. When a social worker thinks of neglect, what comes to his mind is a woebegone, bedraggled child. Technically, however, the law refers to things a parent does or fails to do. If there is an offense, it is the parent's. From that standpoint, the condition of the youngster is evidence against the parent.

This naturally leads to the issue of whether the state of things was deliberately brought about. Especially among people who seldom seem to bring anything to pass deliberately, this is a puzzle. There are those who hold that if the parents are living no better than their child, they cannot be said to be neglecting the child. "You can't prosecute a man for being poor and ignorant." Take, for example, the Smith family.

One has to walk a long distance from either direction to reach the house, since it is far back from the road. Mr. Smith has been building the house himself over a period of years, but the place is still half-finished. After passing through a yard littered with abandoned appliances, discarded auto parts and broken toys, one has to climb over the unfinished concrete foundation of the porch. Two cinder blocks serve precariously as the temporary steps to the front door. The only other exit, through the kitchen, entails a 10-foot drop.

The inside of the house is unfinished plywood, neither walls nor woodwork having been painted. The four-room house is heated by a single

5

wood-burning heater in the living room. Cooking is on a pot-bellied wood burner and a hot plate in the kitchen. The living room is furnished with two overstuffed pieces whose springs protrude dangerously, a couple of wooden folding chairs held together with baling wire, and a creaking rocking chair.

During the interviews, Mrs. Smith would rock and frequently spit snuff drippings into the wood burner. From time to time, she took 18-month-old Joe from his playpen to nurse him. She complained that she had "gone dry", but it was obvious she needed and enjoyed the baby's suckling.

Her 5-year-old, George, was once enrolled in the year-round Head Start program, but Mrs. Smith kept him home after the first few months. At first, she blamed this on a throat infection, later she seized on any excuse she could find. So far as could be determined, it was too much effort for her to get him ready for his ride each morning. She could see no value in his attending preschool each day, although George himself seemed so lonely for companionship that, when in school, he groveled, coerced and begged other children to "be my friend." Later, Mrs. Smith heard of the visiting teacher program and wanted a teacher to come visit George at home once a week.

Paul, the eldest Smith child, is in the 2nd grade, which he attends very irregularly. The mother explains that the other children "pick on him," so her solution is to keep him at home.

During our first home visit, Mrs. Smith had put a frying pan full of grease on the electric burner. Before long, we smelled smoke. The grease had caught fire and ignited towels and diapers that were thrown over a rope stretched over the stove. Mrs. Smith stood clutching the baby, screaming, but otherwise immobilized. The Head Start teacher took the baby out the front door, while the caseworker threw the blazing skillet out the back door and pulled the cloths from the line before the ceiling could catch fire. Throughout all this, Mrs. Smith remained helpless, crying and wringing her hands. Two weeks later, another fire in the living room burned out one whole end of the room.

Of course, the house itself was always cluttered and incredibly dirty. Rubbish was piled in one end of the living room. During one visit, a large rat was observed slipping through the unfinished baseboard and into the pile of trash. The mother remained quite unconcerned, continuing to sit and rock the baby. However, at a later visit, she told of the big rat in the corner they had killed with a broom the week before.

The Smith home is filled with invitations to tragedy: debris in the yard, protruding springs in the chairs, splintered floors, an unprotected rear door, carelessness in handling fire, rats. A report that one of the children had been severely injured would surprise no one who had visited this home. Although such an event might be explained with the saying, "It couldn't be helped," this would not be believable.

Mrs. Smith can be seen as an immature, inadequate mother with emotional needs she is trying to fulfill through her children. She interrupts one child's play to hold him to her dry breast. After allowing George to leave her for a little while, she blocks his continuance in the Head Start program. Paul's attendance in school is at the whim of his child-mother who, in fact, sleeps with the two younger children. All this is known from simple observation. But is it "neglect"? And is it deliberate or "willful"?

In most instances, it is impossible to settle the issue of whether the parents could do better "if they really wanted to." This can be estimated only after treatment is started, and sometimes only after authority is used to challenge them with the threat of removing their children. So in identifying neglect, the focus is on how things have worked out rather than on what the parents intended. Instead of starting with a moral issue, we begin by asking the direct question, "How well cared for is this youngster?"

But measuring the level of child care is still not a simple matter. Many considerations enter in. These include absolutely essential ingredients such as food, housing, clothing, and medical attention, but the child's emotional state is also important, and, in these enlightened times, his need for intellectual stimulation. The sum total of all these things can be referred to as the Childhood Level of Living.

A Childhood Level of Living Scale is presented in Appendix A. It deals with simple, direct facts that a worker would be likely to know about a family, or that she could rather readily find out. The scale is divided into two major sections. The Physical Care Scale deals with the condition of the home, adequacy of food, clothing, furniture, and the like. The Emotional/Cognitive Scale rates the evidences of affection, type of discipline, and cultural stimulation experienced by the child.

From research, there is reason to believe that the child's score on the scale makes a difference in his life. Children scoring at the lower end of the scale were found to average lower in intelligence also. Children from such backgrounds were also more likely to be withdrawn and shy in nursery school, as compared with their peers receiving better care. The scale is not intended as *the* "objective" measure that a worker might bring to court in alleging neglect. But it does guide attention to most of the factors worth considering in assessing a family.

Other findings are helpful. Neglect can be physical or psychological, but in our research among low-income people, the two generally go hand in hand. From a knowledge of the physical care being offered, one may make a fairly accurate guess about the cognitive/emotional care as well. The youngster who is extremely deprived physically but who is said to be well loved and emotionally secure is actually the exception rather than the rule, wishful thinking to the contrary. When the Childhood Level of Living is low in one aspect, it tends to be low pervasively.

Thus, neglect can be identified from at least two angles. One can look at the behavior of the parent—what he does or fails to do. Or one can look at the resultant effects on the child. Some of the effects are urgent. Failure to obtain medical attention for an infected cut or for a case of pneumonia will show up almost at once. There are other more insidious conditions, however, that may not reveal themselves for years. Our research confirms the observation of educators that lack of cultural stimulation is related to lower IQ. Other studies have shown that children fed too little protein in infancy are also likely to emerge intellectually stunted. So even though Mrs. Smith has not abandoned her children and is doing the best she can, the time is fast approaching when the level of care her children are receiving will be regarded professionally, if not legally, as "neglectful."

The Causes of Neglect

What causes child neglect? Why does it happen? These are natural questions in the mind of the child welfare worker. Our work can be steered more intelligently and will have a more lasting impact if it can be directed to rooting out sources of a difficulty, rather than rubbing balm on its symptoms.

There is no one factor that can be said to be *the* cause in every instance of child neglect. So we can only indicate the things that have been most striking in our research. These were: family poverty, and infantile elements in the maternal personality. Most of this book is dedicated to analyzing personality problems among women whose children are neglected, but this emphasis ought not be misinterpreted. On a statistical basis, there is no question that adjudicated child neglect is much, much more prevalent among the poor.

At first glance, the connection of poverty to neglect seems obvious. In the example given earlier, it would seem that if Mr. Smith earned more money, they would have a better house and—at least to some extent—Mrs. Smith's housekeeping problems would be eased. But how is Mr. Smith to get more money? He is a man of limited education and limited energy in a section where even the most competent find it hard to earn much. It seems clear to us that for the Mr. Smiths of this land to be enabled to earn enough to support their families well, we are going to have to modify our methods of distributing income and rewarding work. We take it for granted that without an adequate financial floor under a family the children in it will share a miserable standard of living. There is no mystery about this; much more needs to be done than to be taught. But this takes us into the arena of social action, and that is beyond the scope of this book.

At the same time, we have to recognize that "the poor" are not a homogeneous mass of people, one just like the other. We did one study of 90-odd families, all of whom were below the poverty line, living on AFDC. When all had very similar amounts of money to work with, there were still striking fluctuations in the childhood level of living. It would seem that families in which higher income would make the greatest difference have mothers more competent than Mrs. Smith; given a few appliances, such as a washer and dryer, better housing, continuous hot water, the standards of child care markedly improve. The exhaustion of struggling to make ends meet, living from urgency to emergency—trading off paying the rent against new shoes for two boys, or milk bill against light bill—drains energy that might otherwise be used for motherhood. Yes, food stamp programs and the like can be enormous boons to the children of women who are potentially capable when given a chance. But let us face it: How much income would turn Mrs. Smith into a mature, resourceful and organized person? In our work, it also became clear that there are some mothers who provide for their children at very low standards, but these are no lower than those on which they themselves were reared. Regardless of income, this is all they know about "how one lives."

So we have neglect as a generation-to-generation life style, neglect that comes from sharing family misfortunes in our present society, as well as neglect from the inept use of such resources as there are, due to limitations in the mother. This book is focused almost entirely on the diagnosis and treatment of mothers, but this does not imply that other efforts are not also necessary and useful.

Finally, one may ask why we have not chosen to write about treatment of fathers. The fathers in many of these families make an enormous difference, for good or ill. But on the average, among young children of the low-income family the adequacy of the mother is more crucial. Since we felt this to be so, we focused attention on the mothers involved. One ought to put only so much into any short book. And this one is primarily about mothers.

References

1. Sarah Cleghorn, *The Home Book of Modern Verse*, First Edition, Revised (New York: Henry Holt and Co., 1925), p. 563.

2. Recipients of Public Assistance Money Payments and Amounts of Such Payments, by Program, State and County, February 1970, (Washington, D.C.: Social and Rehabilitation Service, National Center for Social Statistics).

3. David G. Gil, Nationwide Survey of Legally Reported Physical Abuse of Children, paper presented at National Conference on Social Welfare, San Francisco, May 1968.

4. Irving Kaufman, "Psychodynamics of Protective Casework," in *Ego-Oriented Casework: Problem and Perspectives,* edited by Howard J. Parad and Roger R. Miller (New York: Family Service Association of America, 1963), p. 194.

5. Statistics from North Carolina Department of Social Services, Division of Child Welfare, 1970.

6. "In the Interest of Children: A Century of Progress," (Denver: The American Humane Association, Children's Division, 1966), p. 25.

Bibliography

Gil, David G. *Violence Against Children: Physical Abuse in the United States.* Cambridge, Mass.: Harvard University Press, 1970.

Kadushin, Alfred. *Child Welfare Services.* New York: Macmillan, 1967.

Klein, Philip. *From Philanthropy to Social Welfare.* San Francisco: Jossey-Bass, 1968.

Looff, David H. *Appalachia's Children: The Challenge of Mental Health.* Lexington, Ky.: University Press of Kentucky, 1971.

Pumphrey, Ralph E., and Pumphrey, Muriel W., eds. *The Heritage of American Social Work.* New York: Columbia University Press, 1961.

Young, Leontine. *Wednesday's Children: A Study of Child Neglect and Abuse.* New York: McGraw-Hill, 1964.

CHAPTER TWO

Psychodiagnosis

The need for diagnosis stems from the basic nature of our work. We want to make happen those things that will clear up child neglect. However, just as in medicine or auto repair, we first have to determine what is wrong, for leads as to what will make it right. The aim is to help. At the same time, we know we have neither endless time nor enormous power. We have to be efficient in using the resources and abilities available to us. So, in considering the mother, we ask such questions as these:

What about this woman is most worth attending to? Where am I likely to find a clue to what is wrong?

Having decided where the difficulty lies, what actions are likely to bring about change? What is my "theory" about how this woman reacts to things?

Which action that might be taken is within my power? What can *I* do?

When we can answer these questions, we have a psychodiagnosis and a casework treatment plan.

The Process of Psychodiagnosis

Making a diagnosis requires a belief that human behavior forms patterns and a determination to detect them. We begin with somewhat passive observation, taking in as much as we can of the things we have learned that are likely to be relevant. In assessing motivations, we look for recurrences of events, regularities in ways of acting. The next step occurs when we notice that two patterns are not obviously connected, but they might be. Now we are moving from spotting patterns to merging them into larger configurations. And we take a further step, from *"What* does she do?" to *"Why* does she do it?"

Beyond the here and now, of course, is a person with a history. It is usually revealing if we can determine whether the traits a woman is showing are fairly recent or lifelong. Duration helps make clear whether she is reacting to an emergency in her life or showing the basic personality she has always had. In either case, we still have to answer the question, "Why?" but where we look for the answer is very different.

Skill in psychodiagnosis is not something that can be learned from this book, or overnight. It grows during the whole of one's professional working life. But the curiosities remain fairly constant. What are the patterns? Do they make a larger pattern? What do they suggest about what the mother is trying to get for herself and her children, even if she cannot put it into words? How did this urge get started? How likely is she to give it up? Should she give it up, or find a healthy way to satisfy it? What abilities does she have to work with?

There are those who seem to separate making a diagnosis from the process of treatment, but it is only as a convenience for textbook writing or exposition. Actually, the two go hand in hand. When a thoughtful worker is dealing with a client, there is no one point at which he gives up the diagnostic process in favor of full-time engagement in treatment, for there ought to be no point at which observing the client stops. As we look, new facets emerge. Some are new because we did not notice them at first; others, because we were wrong; others, because the client had hidden them; still others, because the client is changing.

It is also true that certain observations cannot be made *until* treatment is attempted. One cannot know how stubbornly a mother clings to the dreadful housing she has until one begins to help her look for better. Only then may it emerge that perhaps she feels she deserves the dilapidated housing she has. As any of us can testify, we do not know how much temper an acquaintance has unless we cross him! In short, the observation that goes on in psychodiagnosis is not a purely passive thing. It includes discoveries that come from small experiments to get the client to change.

If psychodiagnosis means locating patterns among one's active and passive observations of a mother, one still has to choose what to observe. There are, after all, an infinite number of ways one can approach looking at another human being, from the color of hair to the speed and articulateness of speech to the way feelings are expressed. Nor is the child welfare worker a psychoanalyst. The need is for leads about what to look for, aspects that are concrete and that deal with information we are likely to have. A rating system with these characteristics was developed for our research; with a bit of practice, it has been used successfully by AFDC workers.

This instrument is called the Maternal Characteristics Scale and is to be found as Appendix B. It calls attention to a variety of traits and behaviors, and these are significant in making the diagnoses that are presented from Chapter Three onward, where the personality types most prevalent among neglectful mothers are discussed. The worker is urged to sit down with Appendix B and, for the experience, try to complete the scale, keeping in mind one mother with whom he is working.

Verbal Accessibility

There is one dimension of the client's personality we want to emphasize particularly, because it has proved a surprisingly good index both of how intact she is likely to be in general, and how available she will be for casework help. This trait is termed the client's Verbal Accessibility.

Verbal Accessibility is defined as the readiness of the client to talk directly about her most important attitudes and feelings, and to discuss them with her caseworker. Some clients are practically uncommunicative; others talk a great deal, but seldom about anything very personal or important to them. Each of these is in marked contrast to the sort of person who is willing, almost from the first, to tell the worker how she feels, what is really bothering her, what she wants from life.

There are two ways to appraise Verbal Accessibility. One technique is to use a Global Scale. The aim of this scale is not simply to measure verbosity or circumstantiality; rather, the issue is whether the mother will talk meaningfully about her feelings. The scale is:

1. Spontaneous verbalization;
2. spontaneous with caseworker's explicit encouragement;
3. responsive—equal give and take with the caseworker;
4. receptive—little give, lots of take;
5. unresponsive: complete lack of response despite explicit encouragement;
6. avoids or evades verbal expression.

In using this scale, judgment rests on total contacts with the client, whether in one interview or in several. Should a woman score 4, 5 or 6, she would be considered reticent to talk, which would suggest other personality traits associated with verbal inaccessibility.

The other method of assessing Verbal Accessibility is to use the Composite Index. This is done by taking out selected items from the general Maternal Characteristics Scale that are thought to be particularly pertinent to this aspect of the personality. The method of scoring the Maternal Characteristics Scale for Verbal Accessibility is also given in Appendix B. Again, we recommend, for experience, scoring the record of a client one knows well. It is also a valuable way to get a more specific and richer notion of what sorts of behavior the concept of Verbal Accessibility implies.

CHAPTER THREE

Infantile Personalities

It is more or less true that everybody is childlike in some ways. One of the secrets one learns in middle age is that hardly anyone else has grown up completely, either. But when the childishness covers most areas of living and goes to an extreme, we refer to those persons as *infantile personalities,* or persons with a good deal of *infantilism* in their makeup.

Infantilism

All psychotic persons and nearly all neurotic persons show evidences of failure to mature. There are other clients, however, whose problems do not seem to be clearly definable. They have no symptoms, or they have a myriad; they generate troubles for others and themselves; they lack flexibility to adjust to life's crises. Unable to decide just what is wrong, we finally realize that the immaturity is the problem. These are people playing adult roles with the mental and emotional equipment of young children. Of course it does not work. Take this example of two immature people married to each other. As is not unusual, each shows his childishness in a different way from the other.

The Ys are in their mid-30s. Mrs. Y is a housewife; her husband is employed at a local factory. Their four children range from 9 years down to 20 months. Mr. Y manages their money well. They live in a fairly new home and drive a good car. Church-attenders, they are well liked by their neighbors. At first glance, this family has nothing in common with those involved in child neglect.

But behind the lower-middle-class facade there is an emotionally lethal family situation. Mr. Y cannot tolerate the disorganization of his home. The children's loud yelling, his wife's inept fussing, the constant messiness are more than he can stand. So the way he handles it is to come home from work, give all concerned a dose of criticism, and then head next door to work on a dune buggy with his neighbor.

Mrs. Y responds to his neglect by playing Joan of Arc. In fact, she is depressed and has great difficulty getting out of bed in the mornings. When she does get up, she is so disorganized that nothing gets done. The children respond to her helplessness with hyperactivity, commotion, bed-wetting and defiance. They do not undertake even the self-help chores most younger children take for granted.

Neither of the Ys feels adequate to be a parent. Mr. Y has the more socially acceptable line of retreat—he goes to work and otherwise assumes his rights to outside recreation. Mrs. Y has to come face to face with her inability to be a mother. What the Ys have in common are "markedly infantile elements" in their personalities. Even though it would be impossible to charge child neglect in this home, the end result for the children resembles that found in the severe cases from the other side of the tracks.

Infantilism shows itself in a variety of different ways, and how one notices it depends on what aspect of the person's behavior one happens to be conscious of at the moment. Intellectually, for example, such people do not make fine distinctions among their ideas—they can name blue or red, but not lavender or rose. They think concretely, referring to "nickels and dimes" rather than coins, and they may not be able to tell you how a nickel and a dime are alike. They have trouble solving problems, especially when this requires putting ideas into new combinations. And they react in all-or-none terms. You are "good" or you are "bad"—an idea is all right or completely wrong.

In the sphere of the emotions, the infantile person has poor equipment with which to cope with frustration or failure. He gets angry and throws his tools, or he walks off the job and refuses to try again. He may insist that he has not failed at all—that there is nothing wrong with his work. Such explosiveness and impatience make it hard for him to learn complicated skills. Of course, he demands immediate gratification of his wants. He "wants what he wants when he wants it."

Because of their lack of flexibility, infantile women are crippled in handling emotions. This can give rise to psychosomatic illness. If a woman is unable to talk about her disagreements with her husband and iron them out, but can only smolder in silence, it is not surprising that she develops stomach pains or high blood pressure.

Interpersonal Relations

A sphere in which the effects of immaturity are easily visible is in contacts with other people. For one thing, immature mothers often have poor judgment about others. They may trust charlatans blithely, while suspecting those dedicated to their welfare. Sometimes they appear too suggestible; they plead for advice on simple issues. Then they get stubborn and defiant, like a 2-year-old. When the medical care of a child is at stake, such unreasonableness can easily lead to danger.

But perhaps the most characteristic thing about the infantile personality is the way immature persons go about loving. In the love of mature people, there is pleasure in giving as well as in taking. And there is a coming together of two reasonably self-sufficient humans in an attitude that "I could live without you, but I'd much rather live with you." The infantile person, on the other hand, is predominantly self-centered. It is hard for her to care about another for his own sake.

In our society, selfishness is immoral behavior; we look down on it. Actually, it is a misfortune. If a woman is capable of love and sees her child having a good time, she herself is happy, even though nothing special is going on in her own life. In a sense selfishness is bad luck, and such persons are limited to their own tiny worlds and their own senses in order to find pleasure. Sooner or later, of course, boredom sets in. We have to remind ourselves, in diagnosing selfishness, that such a mother did not mean to come out the way she has.

Rather than loving, the infantile woman forms clinging relationships. She clings to her husband in a blind, mutually destructive way; she clings to her children, preventing them from growing away from her. She is happier with a husband who shares enough of her own dependency to reassure her. A man who is mature enough and strong enough to be able to walk away and leave her would frighten her. It is for this reason that it is the rule to find that the neglectful mother has an almost equally immature husband. Sometimes there is so much friction that one wonders why they stay together. But one then realizes that even when they no longer enjoy each other, they cling together out of a mutual dread of loneliness.

Self-Attitudes

It may be helpful to set down the ways such immature people feel about themselves in order to understand them. Here are some things they seem to be saying to themselves:

... I am still a part of my mother; I am incomplete;
... I am fragile, weak and easily damaged;
... I am special, the last baby in the family;
... I am worthless; worst of all, I am unlovable.

It is easy to imagine an immature mother transmitting such attitudes to her daughter, even though they do not logically fit together. When such feelings are transmitted, a generation-to-generation cycle of infantilization has begun. Such a cycle often underlies the more familiar cycle of poverty.

Because of her sense of worthlessness, the immature mother is afraid to ask for love directly, nor will she work at earning it. She demands being met more than half way, with unconditional love. She seems to say, "If you really loved me, you would know what I want without my asking."

Needless to say, almost all severely childish women lack insight as to what is wrong with them. Hardly ever will one seek help to change herself. She comes for assistance, instead, to alleviate the current emergency that she has brought on herself, as often as not, because of her own impulsiveness or self-centeredness.

The Process of Infantilization

Why does this stunting of psychological growth occur? How have these women been infantilized? There is no simple answer, since the process of normal growth requires just the right balance among many different things. A plant may die of drought, but it may also be harmed by too much wetness. So it is with humans.

Some infantile mothers have been overindulged by their own parents, who could not stand the thought of their becoming self-sufficient and able to leave. It is much easier to remain childish, until life catches up with one and suddenly it is a dreadful disadvantage. But for the child, growth requires at least some push or demand by the parents. Overindulgence in specific ways does occur, but it is not the most frequent problem among the low-income women we have been studying.

Infantilization also occurs by identification. The girl may have modeled herself after a mother who was herself a childish woman. Long before we can deliberately select how we would like to be, we are picking up our parents' phrases, their way of walking, their reactions, and the like. So the infantile mother in child neglect may bespeak an immature maternal grandmother, too.

But by far the most frequent cause of infantilism in our women was the massive deprivation in their own lives. Occasionally because she was in a depression, more frequently because of her own inability to give, the maternal grandmother offered minimal child care to the woman of our concern. There was little sensitivity to how she was feeling, no effort made to entertain or stimulate her, often little offered in the way of consistent discipline. The deprivation comes through most graphically in the fact that there was also not enough food or that the food was not there when the neglectful mother felt hungry. From the lack of reliable love and feeding comes the dreadful sense of emptiness. An infant left without milk faces death by hunger or desiccation. And, indeed, most infantile people feel terribly empty, as well as alone. This is one reason they cling; it also accounts for their self-centeredness and demandingness. They do not dare give because their own store of sustenance is so small, and they are desperate in trying to fill themselves.

A number of deprived mothers have also lived through a kind of forced growth that catches up with them only later in life. The eldest child in a large, poor household is first pushed to take care of herself, because "You are my big, big girl!" Next, she is cast in the position of "Mother's little helper." She is already caring for younger brothers and sisters at an age when she really wants to be cared for herself. She enjoys the praise and status of being assistant-mother, but unfortunately, the "maturity" such little girls show at the time is pseudomaturity. Their own childhoods have been skipped, and we have learned that it is really not possible to omit life stages. We often find, in later life, a woman who still resents having to be the "biggest one," and who is competitive with her own daughters. In many respects, she is still as childish as at the point at which she left off in her own babyhood.

Treatment

The treatment of infantile personalities is arduous and time-consuming. Few such mothers "once had it but lost it." Usually they never had it to begin with. What is necessary is to help them acquire in adult life abilities and attitudes luckier people take for granted because they grew up normally. An obvious need is to begin to fill the gaping emptiness that they feel.

These difficulties do not mean that nothing can be done. But they tell us we must be realistic about what is required to bring about real change, and what one can expect from such clients in the meanwhile. We shall discuss such issues as we go on.

For the present, it must already be clear that the nature of the treatment depends in large measure on the specific form that the immaturity takes in a given mother, for there are many ways in which infantilism can show itself. So we move on to our discussion of types of neglectful mothers. Not all of them are infantile personalities, but most have many infantile elements in their personalities.

Bibliography

Hill, Lewis B. "Infantile Personalities." *American Journal of Psychiatry*, 109 (1952), pp. 429-432.

Polansky, Norman A. *Ego Psychology and Communication*. Chicago: Aldine-Atherton, 1971.

Reiner, Beatrice S., and Irving Kaufman. *Character Disorders in Parents of Delinquents*. New York: Family Service Association of America, 1959.

Ruesch, Jurgen. "The Infantile Personality: The Core Problem of Psychosomatic Medicine." *Psychosomatic Medicine*, 10 (1948), pp. 134-144.

Sharlin, Shlomo A., and Norman A. Polansky. "The Process of Infantilization." *American Journal of Orthopsychiatry*, 42 (1972), pp. 92-102.

CHAPTER FOUR

Prevalent Types
of Neglectful Mothers

The types of personalities observed most frequently among mothers in situations of child neglect are:

A. The Apathetic-Futile Mother
B. The Impulse-Ridden Mother
C. The Mentally Retarded Mother
D. The Mother in a Reactive Depression
E. The Psychotic Mother.

The first three categories have many characteristics in common. They have often been lumped together in the literature as *the* neglectful mother. However, they have significant differences as well as commonalities.

The Apathetic-Futile Mother

Identification

Mrs. Cole is a passive woman who shows very little reaction either to the way she lives or to what happens to her. When her husband left her, when her brother was killed in an accident, and when her father died she displayed no outward signs of emotion.

From the time she was first married she has lived in a little house built by her husband and her father on land belonging to her family. Once described as "a cute little place," it is now referred to as a "shack located in the middle of a yard full of debris." The inside of the house matches the filth outside. The children are unbelievably dirty, running through the trash barefooted, frequently getting infections from cuts and scratches.

After completing the 8th grade, Mrs. Cole dropped out of school completely. After she found summer work in a motel, she simply never returned. She worked a year, got married, and has never worked outside the home since. She reads and writes fairly well, and qualified for vocational training when she reluctantly went for testing.

No client has ever been more agreeable than Mrs. Cole; she never argues. In fact, she just does not talk about anything. After 2 years of effort met with her passive, stubborn resistance, her caseworker says, "I just don't get a good picture of her. As a matter of fact, I now hate to go to visit her."

It is probable that every caseworker has encountered more than one Mrs. Cole. She is always at home in body, but there is never any evidence that she has done anything. She may show a flurry of activity—cook a pot of beans or rinse out a few clothes—but nothing really seems worth the effort. And she relates to her family the same way she relates to her worker. She is scarcely aware of the children; her husband, when he stays with her, is given the same low-energy response.

The personality characteristics of the so-called Apathy-Futility syndrome are:

1. A pervasive aura that nothing is really worth doing. These women seldom go after anything with a sense of energy or purpose, and they seem unresponsive to attempts to mobilize them.
2. Emotional numbness, which is sometimes taken as depressiveness but is not so alive as depression.
3. Absence of intense personal relationships beyond a kind of forlorn clinging, even to her children.
4. Expression of anger passive-aggressively, especially in defiance of authority figures.
5. Low competence in most areas, often visibly associated with fear of failure and unwillingness to invest energy to acquire skills.
6. Noncommitment to positive stands and low self-confidence, which contrast with her persistence in stubborn negativism.
7. An almost uncanny ability to infect those who try to help with the same feeling of futility.
8. Verbal inaccessibility regarding important feelings and difficulty in facilitating the thinking through of problems by talking.

It may be hard to distinguish the symptoms of Apathy-Futility from depression. However, in depression the client's feelings are awful, but she does feel. In Apathy-Futility there is numbness. She seems to be saying, "I will feel nothing, and then I cannot be hurt." She is no more able to show love than she is to show real anger. The attitude that "nothing is worthwhile," in other words, is a way of avoiding the involvement that would lead to experiencing her emotions more vividly.

Every human being passes through a stage in which it is necessary to decide, in effect, whether life is worth living; each of us has some capacity to succumb to futility or hopelessness. Therefore the atmosphere these women give off finds echoes in each of us. Besides the frustration we experience when we try to mobilize them to action, their attitude stirs remembrances of our own sense of futility. This is why being around them is so infectious, and why we come to dislike them.

A full-blown case of Apathy-Futility may easily be taken for a case of retardation. However, there are leads in the conversation, such as it is, the the choice of words and the like; we also usually know if a woman, such as Mrs. Cole, can write perfectly well when she wants to. Of course, it is possible to be both retarded and apathetic.

Etiology

How did Mrs. Cole get to be the way she is? By what chain of life events are we now confronted with so lethargic and unmotivated a client? In this instance, there is the advantage of a previous DPW record that tells a long tale of poor education in the grandparents, poverty and alcoholism. For years, they barely managed on the father's small income as a logger. When he retired, he drew an even more limited social security check. Neither of Mrs. Cole's parents had more than a year or so of formal education. Mrs. Cole, her brother and her sister were frequently kept home from school to take care of their inebriated mother or father, or both. Even after the children were grown, they were kept nearby to care for parents who had imbibed too much. None of these children ever broke away. Mrs. Cole married while still young and had five children in rapid succession. Eventually her husband was driven off by her family, even though legally he would be said to have deserted.

Mrs. Cole, with five youngsters, and her unmarried sister, with four, continue to live on the family property. (Mobility is not an outstanding characteristic of those with the Apathy-Futility syndrome.) The brother, who never married, was shot in a neighborhood brawl. The father died recently, leaving his aged widow to carry on, still drinking and still demanding care from her now grown children.

The women we have termed Apathetic-Futile are, in psychiatric jargon, far out on the "schizoid spectrum." That is, they are not schizophrenic, but they are withdrawn and show other disorders. A marked feature is their detachment. They hold back, refusing to invest energy or attention in the world around them.

To understand the feelings of persons who are schizoid, one must go back to infancy, when the infant is completely dependent on his mother.

23

The mother who is the source of the milk of life is, by the same token, the woman who frustrates the infant. This is because even the best of mothers cannot be constantly and immediately available to forestall every need and discomfort her infant may feel. The child's reaction to this is to become angry, for the original purpose of anger is to push the outside world around. Hence, we must surmise that everyone without exception starts life with a mixture of two powerful emotions toward his mother: yearning and anger, or, if you will, love and hate.

If the mother is a dependable, loving person, the child discovers that even if she does not meet his needs immediately, she gets around to him in time. Insecurity gradually is overcome and the child resolves on the side of trust the basic dilemma that Erik Erikson has labeled "trust vs. mistrust." But there are children who are not so lucky, either because they have the sort of mother Mrs. Cole had, or because their otherwise loving and capable mothers were—at the time—in a depression because of the loss of a child or parent, or were ill, or unavailable due to some other life mishap.

There is another important emotion that occurs as a result of deprivation, and the more severe and unrelieved the deprivation, the worse the damage. Deprived infants become depressed. This feeling is likely to remain with them as an undercurrent throughout their lives unless they receive reassurance or compensation for it.

In order to avoid dreadful feelings of depression and anxiety, many such youngsters spontaneously erect a buffer within themselves. They go numb; they refuse to experience emotions at all. You will recall Mrs. Cole's lack of response to the death of her father, the shooting of her brother, the loss of her husband. Persons with this sort of numbness may be said to be detached.

The detachment serves a number of purposes. By refusing to get involved with other people, one escapes the danger of being hurt or of hurting someone. This issue is, of course, very much on the mind of a woman who starts out with such strong feelings of both love and hate against her mother; it is even more of a problem if she is still reacting in an all-or-none way, since the emotions she has are so powerful.

When she begins to love, she automatically feels anger and depression, and anxiety. So she prefers to keep her distance. She may, as did Mrs. Cole, break up her one real love-relationship with a man in favor of a series of one-night stands. Affairs do not make her so vulnerable, because she is less involved. But there are disadvantages, too. In order not to feel hate or depression, the infant, Mrs. Cole, learned to go numb. Now that she is anesthetized, however, life is passing her by, and she feels dead inside, empty, living and yet not living. Her detachment keeps her from forming close relationships, but there is a price for this, also. She is "safe," but she is lonely. There is nothing about Mrs. Cole's shutting the door on pain that promises she will cure her depression, for she has also shut the door on pleasure and enjoyment. No wonder, therefore, that she ends with an overpowering sense of futility. Futility, then, is the predominant feeling; apathy is what we see in behavior.

Results in the Children

What difference will it make for Mrs. Cole's children that she is Apathetic-Futile? At least, she does not treat them as her parents treated her, and she is always with them. It is rare for such a woman to desert. Her type of neglect is more insidious, fostering fairly predictable characteristics in her children. In school the children are seen as withdrawn. They are also more lethargic as 5-year-olds than other youngsters their age. They do not avoid their teacher, but they cling to her. But this is not in real affection, for she discovers they cling to strange adults, too, not out of special attachment but more because of a pervasive panic at being alone. We can only guess how this pattern will look in an older child or adult, but Mrs. Cole may be a fairly good example.

The Apathetic-Futile mother understandably does not have the energy or interest to provide much intellectual stimulation for her child. This showed perceptibly in results of psychological testing. When a mother was seen as highly Apathetic-Futile, her child scored lower than other children in both visual and motor skills. Lower intelligence goes along with having an Apathetic-Futile mother.

It is interesting to note how much of the pattern we are describing has been generally applied to the "cycle of poverty." It is not necessary to be poor, however, to experience the Apathy-Futility syndrome, nor, on the other hand, does poverty immunize one from severe emotional problems.

Treatment

With the high incidence of Apathy-Futility among neglectful mothers, and all-too-familiar results in their children, we are properly charged with responsibility to do something despite their facility at making us feel helpless and hopeless. So far as the child is concerned, removal to a good foster home might seem the answer. But this is not always a ready or available solution. In any case, a useful foster care plan depends on successful involvement of the parent. We are left with no choice but to persist and try to reach the mother. Treating the Apathy-Futility syndrome is usually long, arduous and often unsuccessful. Despite this bleak outlook, some caseworkers who are skilled—and stubborn—continue to achieve results with a good proportion of such women. So there is always some hope for improving the mother's level of operating. In any event, this is a pattern whose depth and rigidity cannot be known until an attempt has been made to help the client change it.

Goals in casework treatment of the Apathetic-Futile client must be set by focusing on one small gain at a time. Self-support and employment for the Apathetic-Futile mother are frequently "paper goals." Typically, she has very little education, she has never held a job outside her home, and she has problems relating to those close to her, let alone an outside employer and fellow workers. One way to spoil any chance of success is by overambitiousness, expecting too much too soon.

The first objective, almost too elementary to mention, is making an initial relationship. A typical Apathetic-Futile mother is reluctant about new attachments because of her fear of how they will work out. The caseworker, therefore, cannot "come on too strong." He must insert himself into her life, but he must be gently intrusive lest he frighten her into retreat. On the other hand, interviews reach a stalemate when the worker himself is so passive he offers no guidance. One way to strike the necessary balance is to be firm and positive about practical things, while being careful not to force the relationship. While one works wholeheartedly to get necessary repairs to her stove or refrigerator, personal feelings between client and worker are left unspoken—in the beginning.

It takes a number of visits for even a very beginning relationship to form; in fact, there is no time over the duration of contact when the worker can take it for granted. Suspiciousness and an urge to withdraw present continuing challenges. Present in the background is the mother's impulse to destroy any growing attachment to another person, and this, too, must be guarded aganist. If for reasons the worker cannot fathom the mother becomes sullen and hostile, it will not necessarily indicate that she dislikes him; it may spring from fear she is liking the worker too much.

The idea of setting goals by mutual agreement may be a good, professional one in most instances. But with the Apathetic-Futile client, it is an empty exercise. Any objectives involving a generally better life must be the worker's, and the client will believe them only after they have been demonstrated. More to the point are basic survival needs with which this mother is familiar, and which she may expect the worker to supply. There is general agreement that one has to do a great deal of concrete giving with most neglectful mothers in the form of money, food and services in the effort to get the family on its feet. This is certainly true with those who are Apathetic-Futile. This kind of concrete helping is a protection to the children, in part; it is also a means of maintaining a relationship with a clinging sort of woman.

Casework treatment techniques so neatly defined in the literature require certain character strengths in the client: desire to be helped; some notion of the kind of help wanted; and the ability to express herself verbally, for casework is a talking treatment. All these abilities are diminished in a woman with the Apathy-Futility syndrome, so of course the usual approach has to be markedly modified. In general, we can say there are three themes in treating her.

First, there is the calculated encouragement of dependency. We try to exploit the client's need to cling, for her own longer-range benefit. Second, there is the emphasis on treatment through increasing the mother's Verbal Accessibility. Both these approaches are described in detail in Chapter Five. Although these techniques are applicable in most cases of neglect, they are especially pertinent to helping the Apathetic-Futile mother.

The third theme is the role of the worker as guide to dealing with the outside world. This mother has multiple limitations, and it is up to her caseworker to supplement her strength as a person, especially in her mental functioning. She may have to be told things she needs to know—such as the fact that some detergents work well with cold water, or that certain diseases will pass from child to child unless precautions are taken. One might have to explain the danger of leaving kerosene or gasoline around in pop bottles, since young children are likely to sample the contents; the worker might have to look over the kitchen with her to shift poisons to the upper shelves. The mother might not realize how much more she can get for her food dollar by shopping in a market rather than buying piecemeal in a quick-shop store. And all mothers are known for the ease with which they can be exploited in exorbitant interest and special charges for credit that they do not immediately comprehend. To point such matters out to her at first will be taken as criticism, but after a relationship is well established, she will welcome the concern.

The worker may have to undertake maternal functions that are beyond the client, for example, dealing with school authorities or discussing pregnancy with an elder daughter. Sometimes the worker has to go with the mother into situations she finds frightening. (Often she will not admit they scare her; she just refuses to have anything to do with them.) This may include driving her chidlren to the clinic, acting as both organizer and social icebreaker for her, and repeating the journey a number of times until she is comfortable enough to set out on her own.

Persons with the Apathy-Futility syndrome are emotionally crippled; all are less effective than they might be, but they vary in their impairment, and therefore in how much help they need. Putting a homemaker into the household is much in order in many instances, either for short-term or long-term "teaching," as a way of *supplementing* a persistently ineffective mother. Finally, if the depth of pathology is such that no improvement is likely, placement of her children is in order. They have to be protected and provided a chance of growing toward a normal life. Here too the worker provides a perspective beyond that of which the client is capable: she is unable to mother, even though she would like to.

The Impulse-Ridden Mother

Early in our work on child neglect it became clear that marginal child care is associated with generalized immaturity in the maternal personality. Then two types of immaturity emerged. In addition to the Apathy-Futility Syndrome, a second group of mothers appeared who were restless and rebellious, seemingly the antithesis of the first.

Yet the two personality types are not entirely mutually exclusive. They shade into each other. We are all familiar with the predominantly lethargic woman who breaks out suddenly into episodes of impulsive behavior. She is the immobilized mother who, all at once, packs and moves into still another dilapidated house, or the withdrawn mother who turns up pregnant when one would have thought she had neither the energy nor the sex appeal to arrange this. On the other hand, the predominantly active mother, always on the go, may lapse into periods of quiet withdrawal not unlike apathy. From experiences like this, we learn that the two types have much in common and even trade symptoms with each other.

There is, however, one important difference between the two. Many of the Impulse-Ridden women are likely to rise to long periods of mature functioning. The Apathetic-Futile mother is rarely capable of performance approximating maturity.

Identification

The outstanding features of the Impulse-Ridden mother are:

She is restless;
she is unable to tolerate stress or frustration;
she is aggressive and defiant;
she craves excitement, movement, change;
she is manipulative of people.

Mrs. Perez was an attractive but physically ailing divorcee who made a comfortable home in a trailer for herself and her two little girls after her husband disappeared. She was friendly with the neighbors and with several male companions. When she dated, a neighbor cared for her children. However, from time to time she did not return when scheduled. Then the neighbor would telephone the caseworker, who would move the children into the already crowded home of their grandparents, where they received care until their mother returned. Sometimes this would be a week later.

Mrs. Perez' escapades have taken her to cities hundreds of miles away.

When she returns, she offers a weak excuse, and then settles down into the role of sweet and competent mother—until the next time.

The impulsive mother is often completely adequate in most respects. She may prepare balanced meals for herself and her children. In our research we found that such women can give thoughtful and appropriate answers to a questionnaire about child-rearing practices. Her problem is not what she knows, so much as what she does. Taking off on an escapade, either with her husband or her boyfriend, is one example. Another is the buying splurge that upsets a whole month's budget. She seems unable to tolerate stable organization or "success" for long.

Impulse-Ridden mothers are found in all walks of life. If the woman is from the middle or upper class, there are usually others in the family and plenty of money to buffer the children against her thoughtlessness. Among the poor, there may be only the neighbors, and it is not uncommon for the police to be called in. Occasionally, even though the mother has a firm resolve to get home within the half-hour, the fact that young children have been left to fend for themselves results in tragedy.

Newspaper stories that report youngsters who have wandered from home and were not missed for a couple of hours, or the death of two infants in a fire while their parents were just down the road disclose instances of this type of mother. These women are typically more capable of emotion than the Apathetic-Futile. Nor are they so tormented about love and hate that they are unable to form relationships. Their problem is that they love, but superficially—like children.

Etiology

Less pervasively damaged than the Apathetic-Futile mothers, the Impulse-Ridden mothers have not undergone so much deprivation in their early childhoods. The critical issue with them is not whether they dare to love; the question is more whether they want to control themselves against strong impulses that strike them, and whether they are able to control themselves when they want to. This involves the process of how limiting behavior is learned.

The infant starts life with the potential for achieving such controls, but does not yet have them. Controls enter the personality by moving from the outside inside. First he goes through the motions to avoid pain; then he goes through them with some resentment, but to keep the love of someone important to him; eventually, however, he does it to please himself and finally he is hardly aware that any control is being exercised. Defiance is not even at issue.

It is extremely important for the young child to feel loved for this process to go smoothly. Otherwise he has nothing to lose by refusing to internalize his parents' standards. Similarly, he will not identify with them—take a model of them inside himself, as it were, in order to keep them close. On the other hand, control systems do not flourish when there is unconditional love. Unless there is effective parental limiting, the overindulged child has nothing to lose. He will not internalize his parents' standards either. Obviously, what is required is a parent who loves, but who also makes demands.

It is also extremely important that the demands experienced by the youngster be consistent. The weak, vacillating mother who sometimes controls and sometimes does not produces a child whose control systems are similarly spotty. This is also true of self-centered parents who "do not love their children enough to fight with them." Indeed, they do not give that much steady attention to the issue of how their children are growing up. Inconsistency also occurs when the two parents are in frequent disagreement about what they want. If mother's signals conflict too much with father's, no firm inner controls are developed.

Finally, one will occasionally encounter persons with surprising backgrounds who seem Impulse-Ridden. One woman, for example, had a father who was very strict and a fundamentalist—she was not allowed to date until she was 16 or 17. In such an instance, we are dealing with an immature conscience. Some women from such families only "behave" under the threat of external pressure. They were so used to "doing what Daddy said" that the controls never became internal, never their own.

Others, however, represent a further complication. They have childlike consciences that operate in stringent, all-or-none fashion. If sex is "bad" it is always bad, even with their husbands. They are so strict with themselves that they permit themselves no fun whatever. For some, such an approach to life becomes intolerable and they kick over the traces; but they go to an opposite extreme. Trying to demonstrate that they are liberated, they want to operate with practically no controls at all. A woman like this will seem highly impulsive. But unlike some others, she becomes guilty about her actions. Unfortunately, her guilt conveniently operates only after she has first had her escapade, so the results in the lives of her children may be the same.

Children with an Impulse-Ridden mother need protection first against the danger and discomfort into which their mother's escapades may bring them. They also need protection against growing up with the same spotty controls as the model before them. In one study we found that youngsters, even at age 5, showing hostile-defiant behavior had mothers rated high on impulsivity—a seed bed for later delinquency.

Treatment

In a general way the treatment of the impulsive mother follows from knowledge of the way her difficulties got started. We seek to establish a relationship with her in which, as she comes to like and depend on us, our opinions matter to her. We then can use this leverage to encourage her to put limits on herself—first, perhaps, primarily to please us, but gradually in order to please herself. We try to help her see how her behavior creates unpleasantness for herself as well as her children. One emphasis is on her wants, her needs, as she prefers, with the aim of teaching her to delay her rush toward gratification for the sake of more satisfaction in the long run. The other emphasis is on helping her learn to "talk it all out rather than act it out." These are the principles. The practice is not easy. However, the worker is supported by the knowledge that others have had success with many Impulse-Ridden mothers.

Even though the impulsive mother is oriented to action rather than talking, or experiencing feelings, she usually has little trouble verbalizing her needs and wants. In fact, impossible demands on the worker, followed by righteous indignation if they are not met, are not at all uncommon. Her manipulations can be annoying when they are obvious, but some are so adroit that it is intriguing to try to keep up with them.

One woman was never at home when her worker was supposed to visit, but she would leave behind broad hints with a neighbor as to where she would be. The worker then tracked her down, and took her home where he could talk with her. His persistence in the face of her testing was finally rewarded when she stayed home to meet him, and told him that she had discovered that he really was on her side and wanted to help. Irritation with such ploys is alleviated when we stop regarding the client as a mother aged 25 or 30, but think of her behavior as that of an unruly child somewhere between 3 and 9.

That these mothers are unmotivated for treatment is inherent in their problems. Before the caseworker expects anything as organized as a client's desire to change herself, the first goal is simply to get involved, and go on from there. Contrary to gentle intrusiveness with the apathetic woman, here the worker's aim is to present himself as a person of strong character, unlikely to have his feelings hurt by the avoidance or demanding outbursts of the client. This does not mean being "hard," for the sense of caring for the client must also come through. But in the face of her manipulativeness, she will feel safer dealing with someone who is sturdy and not easily hurt or dismayed. The reason for one's entering the situation should be stated clearly and placidly.

There is always the question of what point to begin to try to introduce some controls. The minor manipulative tactics present relatively little problem from this standpoint. Almost from the beginning, it is all right in most instances to confront her with, "Well, I guess you really don't want to see me," or "Do you want me to chase you to find you?" and the like. On the other hand, confronting her about her major indiscretions takes finesse. If one lets oneself sound moralistic—and one may, of course, be shocked at something she has done—one only allies oneself with the other complaining authorities she has spent a lifetime teasing. A better tack is to concentrate on the disadvantages of her behavior to her, which is what is really most on her mind. It is as well if such reminders occur in the context of a relationship in which concrete assistance to the client has already been given. Once the client has some liking for the worker and has demonstrated need of him, her behavior and its consequences for her and for her children should be frankly discussed.

Eventually, as all experienced workers know, it is possible to have so strong a relationship with an impulsive mother that even an open quarrel is acceptable to her. This occurs in a setting of trust and intimacy, as it would in a family, in which the quarrel is truly about whether what she has done is to her own best interests.

The purpose of treatment is to reduce the confusion and frustration that drive this mother to do what she has been doing. We accomplish this by offering ourselves as teacher—and as models. We hope she will find better ways to manage her energies, so that the momentary fling does not reduce the chance for pleasure over the long run. Not many of these women develop insight. They do not think of themselves as "changing"; just of getting what they want in a smarter way. If her behavior has changed, one should not insist that her words change, too.

The Mentally Retarded Mother

Another group of concern to caseworkers includes those mothers whose inadequacy stems from below-average intelligence. Not only is the care the retarded mother gives her children pervasively poor, but she herself is a limited target for casework treatment. How can we help?

In the field of mental retardation, confusion arises because terms are bandied carelessly about and generally misunderstood. We talk of feeble-mindedness, mental deficiency, mental subnormality, mental retardation, or borderline retardation as if they are synonymous. Even if the terms were used precisely, one cannot apply them to draw conclusions about a mother without considering what she is actually doing or not doing for her children.

From those who have done extensive psychological testing of mothers in poverty families, we have learned that the average IQ of such mothers falls typically in the borderline range of 68 to 83. In our own study of the self-supporting poor, the average IQ of the mothers was 79. Although this indicated that the thinking capacity of many—by no means all—was severely limited, we found that the quality of the care given the children does not seem to be grossly affected until the mother's score drops below 70. Inadequate and neglectful care may be expected when the IQ of the mother is below 60.

The American Association on Mental Deficiency has given the following guidelines to estimated degrees of intelligence:

Borderline Retardation	IQ 68—83
Mild Retardation	IQ 52—67
Moderate Retardation	IQ 36—51
Severe Retardation	IQ 20—35
Profound Retardation	IQ below 20

Our discussion will be confined to mothers who fall into the categories of borderline, mild and moderate retardation. Within each group, abilities vary widely, and individual potentialities for mothering and learning must be assessed. But we are reminded again of the reluctance of caseworkers to look at the negatives among those they are trying to help. Often the worker assumes personal responsibility for the lack of progress and refuses to see a situation as inevitably irreversible. While making every effort to help her, the worker must maintain skepticism about how much his services to a retarded, neglectful mother can help the children. Such a mother may be able to learn simple tasks—but adequate mothering is not a simple task.

Retarded mothers in the borderline range perform much like an average 10-year-old child. Those with greater retardation function at correspondingly younger levels of development—even to preschool or kindergarten performance. Mothers suffering from emotional immaturity or conflict may sometimes give the impression that they are retarded. However, they score higher in intelligence testing and may be spotted by caseworkers through the simple criteria suggested in the following section. On the other hand, mentally retarded women often have emotional problems and distortions similar to those of women of average intelligence. It is possible to be both retarded and emotionally disturbed.

Identification

Formal intelligence testing of all applicants as a criterion for service is neither tactful nor practical. However, clues are frequently available to help the caseworker assess the level of intellectual functioning of the individual client. School records sometimes include results from earlier testing. A history of placement in a special education program or a state institution for the retarded suggests limitations. Reports from family and acquaintances about a mother may alert the caseworker to the possibility that retardation is a cause of her difficulties. In that event, major life decisions should not be made about a mother and her family on the basis of presumed mental retardation. It is imperative and professionally ethical that valid, competent psychological testing be carried out.

Immature cognitive development manifests itself in a variety of ways. The following symptoms are not to be taken as definitive, but will alert the caseworker to the probability of retardation:

1. Illiteracy in women is almost invariably associated with significant mental retardation. Some retardates are able to read safety signs and simple directions, but few can comfortably read newspapers or magazines, instructional pamphlets, recipes, or manuals on welfare rights. Most retarded women will be able to print their names and maybe a few simple words, but cursive writing, if they can do it at all, will be done slowly and awkwardly.
2. Some are able to tell time accurately, while others can tell time only to the hour or not at all. Calendars are confusing to many borderline retardates. For those with lesser ability, the seasons are judged by the weather or such activities as planting in the spring, raking leaves in the fall.
3. If the retarded mother can count and identify bills and coins correctly, this will probably be the limit of her skill in money management. She relies upon more competent people to assist her, and she depends upon the good will of merchants not to cheat her.
4. The thinking of the retarded person is almost always characterized by excessive concreteness and rigidity. That is, they have trouble seeing relationships between objects or events. They can focus their attention on only one thing at a time; they have "one-track minds."
5. Most retarded persons are able to travel over familiar routes, get about a small town, use the local shopping centers. However, the unfamiliar is frightening to them, and they must depend upon others to get them where they need to go.

With the development of centers for training and teaching retarded children, many of the retarded mothers coming to our attention have had schooling in one of these centers and have continued until they "aged out." Those who have had only public school opportunity will possibly get through the 6th grade, if social promotion is practiced. Often they will have stayed in school until they reached the minimal age limit of 16, and then quit.

A few borderline retarded women have held employment. They have been known to work successfully in routine, unskilled jobs such as packaging, simple assembly, or food processing. Frequently they are hired by other mothers as low-cost baby sitters. For obvious reasons, this practice should be discouraged. The retarded woman should also be discouraged from taking a job that is too complicated or involves skills that she can never acquire. Failure only adds to her long experience of frustration and discouragement.

Manual skill is not usual in the retarded woman. She typically lacks the ability to operate or maintain complicated machinery or appliances. Washing machines, vacuum cleaners, sometimes even stoves baffle her. This accounts for the short life of labor-saving devices in her home.

Childlike and naive, these mothers are highly suggestible and easily influenced. They often are vulnerable to being exploited or cheated. One woman who lived with her baby in the home of her stepmother was made to do all the housework for a family of nine. Two retarded sisters, who lived together with their children, were good workers in a nursing home. When they applied for AFDC, despite an income of over $500 a month, it was found that each week they made payments on 14 insurance policies!

We see also manifestations of intellectual handicap in the recreation of the retarded. They seem to prefer activities expectable among grammar school children. Mothers severely retarded are often found playing with dolls or coloring books, or engaging in other preschool hobbies.

The concreteness of thinking in the retarded woman leads her to have difficulty in making appropriate adult judgments. She is not likely to notice the early symptoms of illness in a child or to relate these to treatment. She cannot be relied upon to follow through on medical directions when the child is ill, nor can she anticipate dangerous situations.

The children of Mrs. Jones were often exposed to hazards. Her 3-year old son Philip was left to play barefoot in the mud puddles around the trailer home while all around him were jagged bits of metal broken off from rusty car fenders, and pieces of shattered glass. When her daughter Angie became seriously anemic, iron tablets had to be given by the Head Start teacher. Mrs. Jones could not remember to give the medicine daily. Moreover, she could not think of Angie as ill—she was "just a little pale."

The Jones baby, an 18-month-old toddler, was found at home almost unable to breathe because he had packed bits of paper and food deep into his nostrils. His mother had not noticed. The Head Start teacher had also reported extensive body-rash on all the children from insect bites. Mrs. Jones said she wanted to get rid of the bugs and agreed to be home the next day when the man from the Health Department planned to exterminate. But the following day the trailer was locked, and no one was at home.

Etiology

An individual unfamiliar with retardation may picture a person with a physically distorted figure, with a disproportionately large or small head, misshapen skull, dwarfism or giantism, visual astigmatism, unsightly orthopedic conditions, and so forth. Such conditions are usually accompanied by permanent severe, organic impairment of the central nervous system. Women so handicapped are usually protected by life-long custodial care within their families, or they are placed in institutions. Rarely do we find one, nowadays, parenting a child.

The mother we see who is intellectually limited, therefore, often has the physical appearance of a normal adult. Her problem does not indicate great damage to the central nervous system. Such a mother was often not recognized as retarded until she started school. The exact cause of the retardation is often never established. More often than not, the poor, neglecting retarded mother is reflecting her own barren upbringing—poverty, lack of stimulation, limited opportunity for social interaction, and a series of self-defeating failures. She probably grew up with the kind of haphazard care she now gives her own children. Often she is herself a neglected child grown up, a product of cultural deprivation. In some instances, however, the social history will show that the mother began her own life as a premature baby, or with severe illness in infancy.

Among the mothers we see it does not matter greatly whether the retardation was due in the first place to a depriving environment, to poor heredity, or to central nervous system disease. By the time the retarded child is half-grown, her limitations become essentially less reversible. We cannot realistically hope that pouring in stimulation in adulthood will improve basic functioning. It will be too little; it is already too late. Our problem, rather, is to discover the limits of the mothers' abilities to care for their children, and try to help them reach these. The biggest thing we learn from trying to puzzle out the cause of the retardation is the desirability of not letting it go on to the next generation.

Effects on the Children

What happens to a child who is cared for by a Mentally Retarded mother? First, his physical survival through infancy is precarious. Without the assistance of more adequate relatives or other adults, the retarded mother cannot meet the needs of the infant, whose very life depends upon regular nourishment and protection from cold and other dangers.

Before Johnny Adams was 3 months old, he had been hospitalized five times with illnesses related to exposure and inconsistent care—pneumonia, malnutrition, etc. It seemed that Mrs. Adams, deserted by her husband before Johnny's birth, would not get up during the night to stoke the fire in the little wood stove that heated the drafty shack. The fire went out. She stayed warm under piles of old quilts, with no thought of the uncovered infant in his crib. She also could not remember to give him his bottle on any schedule. Johnny was wasting away, an example of "failure to thrive."

The retarded mother quickly forgets anything out of sight. A projected quick trip to the store can last for hours if she is diverted along the way.

Little Bertha was placed in her playpen in the sun before Miss Ray left for the store. After all, the pediatrician had told her that the baby needed sunshine. Hours later a neighbor heard the whimpering of the suffering infant and took her to the hospital, where she required treatment for serious burns over most of her body. Miss Ray had been enjoying herself, drinking a soda, being with people in the neighborhood grocery store. She was never quite able to understand what had happened, since she was "just following doctor's orders."

Our concern for the child of the retarded mother increases as we learn more about the necessity of proteins in the development of brain tissue. If no thought is given to the child's nutritional needs, but he is fed at the whim of a child-mother, eating only the foods she likes, nourishment for his body and mind is a matter of chance. And the chances are poor.

The failure to provide food is matched by the retarded mother's inability to provide cognitive stimulation. We can expect a repetition of the cycle of school failure, social ineptness, and eventual retardation, not necessarily because of inherited characteristics, but because of environmental stimulus deprivation. Language development is likely to be slow. As the child grows older, his problems are likely to become increasingly serious as he lives from day to day with immaturity and child-like behavior of a parent who cannot function as an adequate model. The mother's own simplistic beliefs, superstitions, even her verbal expressions, become a part of his "education."

It is difficult, if not impossible, for the Mentally Retarded mother to become an effective influence on the behavior and character of her children as they grow older. Discipline is likely to be either nonexistent or harsh, inconsistent, unrelated to the behavior in question, and inappropriate to the child's age. The retarded mother's responses are rigid and usually reflect blind adherence to what someone has told her is right or wrong.

Treatment

Mentally Retarded mothers usually require some supervision in the management of their affairs, including child care. Sometimes this help is provided, more or less effectively, by their own parents or other more competent relatives. The caseworker needs to work with both the retarded mother and those who are exercising the supervision. There is a temptation to bypass the retarded mother and deal only with more competent relatives. But respect of the feelings of the retarded mother and involvement of her in plans are extremely important to success.

There are many retarded mothers who are trying to rear their children without help except that offered by the caseworker. One of the first requirements will be that workers understand early in the relationship what the diagnosis of mental retardation means with respect to the limits this imposes upon the kind of help such a mother can use and the rate of progress, if any, that can be anticipated. This is one situation in which it cannot be hoped that things will improve. Passage of time often means that the child is losing precious ground in his development.

Take, for instance, the earlier account of Mrs. Adams and Johnny. During the first few months of Johnny's life, the pediatrician telephoned the social services department, suggesting that a foster home be found for the baby. After much wheel spinning at the agency, Johnny became 6 months old and "didn't look neglected." He was being fed regularly, the same diet his mother had, biscuits, gravy and soda pop. Now, 2 years later, there is concern because Johnny has not said one word. He is a dull, lethargic child whose retardation may be irreversible. We are not suggesting that had Johnny been placed at 3 months of age he would become a whiz kid; but we are predicting that, being left with his mother, he will carry on the familial pattern of retardation.

The question of placement for children of retarded mothers should be considered as early as possible, not deferred in hopes that casework treatment of the mother will make such consideration unnecessary. Often the essence of casework, talking, cannot even be used effectively. The caseworker must develop skills to demonstrate what needs to be done, instead of talking about it. He must exercise authority firmly, but kindly. One never "suggests" to the retarded mother, but one does say firmly, "This must be done, and this is the way to do it."

How can this be done without raising a solid wall of childish resistance and stubbornness? We treat them as the children they are. They understand kindness, attention, simple language, one-at-a-time directions, honesty, praise and rewards. We must win their affection so that we can influence their behavior—make them want to please us.

If the decision is made that the children are to remain with the intellectually limited mother, it must be understood that the caseworker's responsibility increases. Beyond providing basic necessities, he will be involved in many areas of the client's life, especially where the welfare of the children is concerned. Since money management is a chronic problem, these mothers need specific help in shopping for food, clothing, furniture— not just a demonstration trip, but routinely. Extreme cases of financial incompetency may require the appointment of a personal representative to control all expenditures.

The caseworker will have to arrange transportation for medical or other needed services if the mother must leave familiar surroundings. He will have to be responsible for the mother's keeping appointments at the right time on the right day. Generally, it is advisable to remind her of an appointment the day before, or even the same day, if possible. Relating an appointment hour to some routine in her life helps her get ready on time—e.g., "I'll pick you up right after the school bus leaves with the children" has more meaning than, "Be ready to go at 8:30 in the morning."

Responsibility for keeping an eye on the medical needs of the retarded mother and her children can be shared by the caseworker and the health department. Regular visits by a public health nurse may be desirable to catch symptoms of illness early. The mother needs to be reminded by someone to get immunizations for the children as they are due. Constant check on what is fed and when to feed the children, especially babies under 2, will be one of the most important and difficult functions of the nurse or caseworker.

Clothing children is usually left to the discretion of the mother, if she is at all competent. But with the retarded mother there will be little awareness of when clothing needs replacing, and she will probably not have the ability to make alterations or repairs. She may be able to dress the children appropriately for the weather conditions, but even this should be checked.

One of the most helpful services to the retarded mother would be a homemaker, with understanding and qualifications to take over. Sometimes the homemaker can demonstrate domestic procedures. But we must accept the reality that the more retarded mothers will need constant supervision and their children will need a substitute mother until they are grown.

The greatest concern in regard to the retarded mother is the lack of emotional cognitive nurturance of her children. The earlier they can be exposed to more healthy, stimulating social and educational experiences outside the home, the better. Nurseries, Head Start (sometimes too late), day care centers, or any approved program the community has should be used to compensate for what the children miss from their mothers. The caseworker should help the older children become involved in recreational facilities, scouting, big sister or big brother organizations. The total community should be aware of, and when possible involved in, appropriate ways for helping the family.

Many communities have developed programs for the retarded adult, as well as for children. Some of these are purely social, while others offer training in self-help, grooming, hygiene and protection. The caseworker involved with a retarded mother and her family should become familiar with community resources, and even encourage the formation of groups to meet needs, if she has several women with this problem.

The Mother in a Reactive Depression

An important point to clarify in assessing any new case of child neglect is how long it has been going on. If it represents a sharp change from the mother's usual behavior, it may tell us that she is depressed.

By the term "reactive depression" we refer to a cluster of feelings and behaviors that are morbid or unhealthy, reactions to the loss of a loved person, or to other kinds of traumatic life events. It is called "reactive" depression because it is in reaction to a specific external stimulus and is distinguished from depression that seems to arise from deep, long-standing processes within the person.

We in social work see a great many depressed people. This is because the amount of bad luck and traumata experienced by some of our families is almost unbelievable to those who have not shared their lives.

Mr. D, age 46, had been an independent man, a skilled textile worker for most of his adult life. In the course of a routine physical examination, he was told that tests indicated he had tuberculosis, although the affected area could not to be identified. Therefore, he could not return to his work. But, pending a definite diagnosis, he was not eligible for compensation, nor did he have a sufficiently well-defined disability to make him eligible for public assistance.

Mrs. D, 45, had been hospitalized for tuberculosis 12 years previously. In her, the disease was arrested, but she remained frail and had difficulty holding a job outside the home while caring for three children.

Adding to the strain imposed on the family by the sudden loss of income was the vagueness about Mr. D's diagnosis. Meanwhile he was subjected to a battery of examinations, including bronchoscopy, broncho-grams and the like. A sense of impending disaster began to develop in Mr. D, a kind of anticipated mourning response. Desperate for income, he turned to driving a cab, concealing his doubtful medical history. One Sunday morning their 15-year-old son Larry, on a sudden impulse, decided to drive his father's cab to church as a prank. When Mr. D discovered the loss, he immediately notified the police, but Larry had already driven the car into a ditch.

In this instance, the juvenile law worked swiftly and Larry was sent to training school. There disaster compounded disaster, like a Greek tragedy. While on work detail in the laundry, he either fell or was pushed into an open industrial washing machine and was killed. The father invoked a life insurance policy on the boy that was in good standing, and made arrangements for the funeral. But before the boy's body had left the funeral home, the insurance company notified the Ds that "by virtue of institutional placement, Larry was not a member of the household at time of death" and so no benefits were payable. The boy's body was transferred into a pine box provided by the county.

A week after the funeral, Mrs. D suffered a recurrence of tuberculosis symptoms that had been dormant for 12 years. Her weight dropped to 90 pounds; a bronchial cough and other respiratory symptoms developed; she began to cough blood. Yet all X-rays remained negative, and no physical basis for the symptoms could be established. Mrs. D went into a deep depression, refused to wear any clothing but her robe and slippers, and spent entire days in bed, as if back in the sanitarium. Mr. D sat on the couch in the living room, alternately immobilized by despair and raging against all authorities—court, institutions, welfare workers, hospitals, doctors, insurance companies, and those he was convinced killed his son.

During this time, the two younger children were fed, clothed and kept in school by neighbors. Mr. and Mrs. D stated that they would just sit at home and die, since evidently the whole community just "wanted to kill them off." In one effort to seek redress, Mr. D. went to the Juvenile Court. There he was told that some children are born good and others born bad, and Larry was just one of the latter. This did not seem to help him.

Normal Grief Reactions

Reactive depression is not to be confused with the varied but still normal ways in which grief can be expressed at the time of a shock, separation or death of a loved one. The free expression of anguish, self-reproach, irritation is to be encouraged at such times. Indeed, difficulty occurs when these feelings are not expressed, because such suppression distorts the normal process of grieving. Then the feelings may emerge much later, displaced and twisted, in the form of a stubborn reactive depression. Erich Lindemann has given us a comprehensive description of expectable mourning processes. These include such temporary, but only temporary, symptoms as:

1. Bodily distress with disturbances in breathing, digestion and feelings of weakness and exhaustion. Tightness in the chest and literally a pain in the heart will be present.
2. Feelings of depression, with a sense of unreality and of emotional withdrawal from other people and events.
3. Intense preoccupation with images of the deceased.
4. Feelings of guilt about possible negligence, and regret that more was not done for the deceased person.

5. Temporarily impaired relationships to other people, with anger, irritability and hostility, and disorganized activity in general.

The resolution of grief in normal mourning occurs through what has been well called "grief work." We lean on the friends who come to call. We revive and live through again the memories associated with the loved ones we have lost. We go through the agonizing "work" of funerals, burials, disposition of effects, care of mementoes and photographs, settling estates and the like. Through release of feelings, through dependency on other loved ones, we express our grief. The completion of rituals gradually reassures us that we have been responsible and devoted. The pain of memory gradually recedes, and the attachment to the one we loved is loosened until it is relinquished. Thus, the wound is bound and heals itself. The grief, and its temporary depression, are said to be "self-limiting." Normally, that is, they clear by themselves.

But sometimes when a mother appears withdrawn and indifferent, she is overwhelmed and immobilized by despair from a loss no one has helped her to work through. She may still be responding to an event that happened long before, since many cases of reactive depression are left untreated and become worse. Of all the conditions we are considering in this book, this one is most likely to respond to casework treatment; and among our clientele depression is highly prevalent.

Identification

The Mother in a Reactive Depression may be immobilized; behavior that otherwise looks like indifference or apathy is actually severe reaction to loss of the loved person. Typically there is a persistent mood of despair and sadness; a sense of impending doom; slowing down of behavior and thought processes; some inability to concentrate; indecisiveness so that the client, by herself, is unable to seek help. Insomnia and "early waking" are the marks of mild depressions, as are often loss of appetite and constipation. Sometimes, however, the depression shows itself in more severe psychosomatic complaints such as asthma, colitis or other physical diseases triggered by emotional problems. Lindemann, again, gives us additional points to look for in identifying reactive depression;

1. Reaction to the life event may be delayed or postponed. The client seemingly retains her morale for weeks or months, but a reactivation may be suddenly precipitated by some other, less important, life happening.
2. There may be frenzied overactivity. Clients are also known who have adopted the symptoms shown by the deceased during his last illness, or they show other medical problems.

42

3. Withdrawal of attention to family and friends, and general social isolation often occur, accompanied by general loss of initiative.
4. There are outbursts of fury against specific persons, such as doctors and surgeons. Almost anyone who becomes deeply involved with the bereaved person becomes liable to attack, as her dependency on him reminds the mother of her dependency on the one she has lost.
5. Strong feelings of guilt and self-destructive behavior occur. Sometimes there is a suicide attempt. The mother may debase herself, seemingly deliberately, involving herself sexually with inappropriate men or refusing to "fix herself up" or being unwilling to "give herself the satisfaction" of enjoying a new dress, a hair styling, even a good home.

A good social history gives us many clues to identification of a reactive depression. In fact, the effort to get such a history from the client is often, in itself, useful therapy. To repeat, when a mother who had previously given good care rather suddenly shifts to slovenliness, we may well ask whether we are witnessing an instance of a person suffering from unresolved grief.

Etiology

We have been describing depression primarily as a reaction to loss of someone who is loved—a dreadful life event that is vivid and understandable. Let us take note of two further considerations. First, loss of a loved person is, of course, not the only thing that triggers depression. Second, although terrible events can easily lead to depression, most people actually shake it off spontaneously rather soon, and go on. In other words, people vary in their ability to roll with the punches.

According to the classic explanation, depression is anger turned against oneself. The woman is hurt by some person or tragedy; the hurt leads to anger, an automatic response over which she has no control. She punishes herself out of guilt for being angry and as a substitute for pounding the the person she cannot or dare not hit. One of the ways she punishes herself is by feeling badly; she also feels anxious for fear she will lose control and strike out in anger; and she is prone to downgrade and deprive herself as punishment.

Take the case of the woman whose husband has died. It is not uncommon to hear, among the tears, such recriminations as, "How could you go away and leave me?" Obviously, she is angry at the one who has deserted her. But this is a ridiculous feeling, to her adult mind, and also adds to the guilt she already feels toward the deceased person. It is no wonder, therefore, that it is so rare to find a bereaved person fully conscious of the anger they feel toward the one who has died. It is generally not easy to get the rage of depressed persons out in the open, and only highly skilled people should try. But the generalized irritability that so frequently accompanies depression is more understandable if we accept this picture of what goes on.

Of course, what makes the mother depressed is not the fact that she is so filled with anger and desire for vengeance. The depression comes from the fact that she is also a decent person, capable of feeling guilt, and reluctant to strike out at someone she has loved.

What are some other events that lead to depression? Drastic illness, a brush with death, is one. Under these circumstances, the woman who is ill faces the prospect of losing not just one person, but everybody! Depressions also occur in reaction to crippling mishaps, such as loss of a limb or disfigurement. It is possible to be in mourning for oneself—"The me I used to know and love is gone." Consider the blow it must be to a man who has always enjoyed his strength to be afflicted with a chronic illness such as heart disease. One also sees depression in reaction to failure, with the implication that one is not much of a person. A deserted woman will say bluntly that she would have preferred that her husband died than that he left with another woman; the desertion is a blow to her self-esteem.

Why are some people more prone to depression than others? Part of the answer we already know from our discussion of normal processes of grief work. Those who can face their feelings and get them off their chests are better protected against lingering depressiveness. People who are ashamed of expressing feelings, who bottle up their emotions, are at a disadvantage. They pay a price for rigidity. For in bottling up the anger, they do something else they had not counted on. The anger remains suppressed, but so do the other emotions, such as joy and pleasure and loving. All that comes out is irritation with life.

Unwillingness to express emotions is partly dependent on the cultural background. There are many parts of the rural South, for example, in which demonstrativeness is more or less forbidden by the code. But even in nondemonstrative cultures, there are still noteworthy differences among families. It pays, therefore, to look into the family pattern. Sometimes we find that the mother has no reservations about letting her feelings out, but no one has cared enough to listen.

Effects on the Children

A mother suffering from reactive depression may expose her children to all the hazards of child neglect. When one mother was unable to leave her bed, even the physical needs of her children had to be assumed by her neighbors. Another woman, who took large amounts of medication and made recurrent suicidal gestures, so disregarded her youngsters that they had to be placed with relatives.

The underlying sadness in the depressive mother leaves her unable to communicate to her child feelings of joy, wonder, excitement, curiosity or even love. This gives him a legacy of constrictedness and guilt, if he identifies with his mother and takes over parts of her personality into his own. And, of course, a woman in a depression is in poor position to fulfill the role of mother. Some of the women we described as showing the Apathy-Futility syndrome were the products of unrewarding infancies because their own mothers, in turn, were depressed. A depressed woman cannot respond sensitively to her infant's needs because she is oblivious to his signals. She is also unable to offer the warmth and service all of us need to reassure us that the world is not such a bad place after all.

Older children whose mothers become depressed also show evidence of disturbance. The youngest child in one family went through a phase of restlessness and irritability in school at the time her mother was in her worst state. We should not lose sight of the need to help these mothers see that their children, too, need to learn to express feelings honestly. Nor should children be shielded from all suffering. This is not reality, either.

In many instances the child will have to be removed from his neglectful mother. And although she may be inadequate, she is the only mother he has known. Consequently, mourning reactions are to be expected from children who have had to be removed, even for their own good. Our openness and sympathy may help the child carry out the necessary grief work when the separation is still fresh. In that way, we have a better chance of warding off resentment and depressiveness that he might otherwise carry into his adult life.

Treatment

The treatment of reactive depression involves two major themes: ventilation and restitution. By "ventilation" we refer to helping the mother "air her feelings," get her grief and anger off her chest by expressing whatever seems to need expressing, even if it does not seem to her, or to us, to make a great deal of sense. Part of the treatment is already under way as we begin to learn what has been going on, and why she feels so badly.

By "restitution" we have in mind processes of making up to her for what she has lost. In the case of a death this is, of course, not literally possible. But it is true that one cure for losing a loved person is to find another. The caseworker, with his attentiveness, interest and concern, compensates in part for the loved person who is gone. Naturally, this is only a temporary arrangement. Our job is to help her over the crisis so that she can go on and hopefully find others with whom to make compensatory attachments. Restitution also includes making up for the hurts in other ways, as in the process of normal "grief work."

In the D family treatment consisted, first, of allowing for outpouring of all the anguish associated with such a horrible series of events. Once rational elements could be separated from the unreasonable, Mr. D was supported in seeking redress. As a beginning, the caseworker accompanied him to the state training school, where a sympathetic superintendent allowed him to visit the laundry and relive, step by step, the events leading to his son's death. They admitted blame in that no adult had been present while the boy was working around the huge, uncovered washing machinery. Mr. D located a lawyer willing to investigate his seeking legal redress for his son's death. The caseworker was also able to get state office intervention to clarify procedures so that public assistance could now be granted the family.

As Mrs. D became more able to talk, she revealed the accidental death some 12 years earlier of another son, then aged 3. He had been playing on the sidewalk when a car left the street and killed him. His mother had been ironing at the time and was filled with self-reproach for his having wandered unsupervised into the yard. The same feelings were triggered again, and this time she blamed Mr. D for not having fought the court harder to keep Larry out of the institution.

Mr. D was also angry with himself for allowing the judge to persuade him that Larry needed such stern disciplining. He had a grudge against his wife for having overprotected Larry, as her favorite child, feeling that this led to his prank. Both parents now were making comparisons between Larry, an A student, and a younger brother who seems slow, but who survived. So the depression into which Larry's death had sent them was a blow with a history that made it worse.

After months of grief work and steps seeking the righting of injustices that had been done, the Ds emerged with much of their original resilience. Mrs. D took a position as a practical nurse in a convalescent home, thus sublimating the sort of needs that led her to take to her own bed the year before.

More cruelty lay ahead for this family. The following year, Mr. D's condition was finally diagnosed as lung cancer, and he died in his wife's arms after surgery. A noted surgeon wrote a letter of great humility apologizing for the delay in diagnosis and the many difficulties Mr. D had undergone. This time, Mrs. D underwent a period of normal grief work. She is now operating at a mature level as a productive worker and a good mother. She refers many cases to the agency.

In this one case we see all the characteristic behavior patterns of reactive depression, including Mr. D's being in mourning for himself. We also see the roles that ventilation and active seeking of restitution can play in lifting the depression. As the depression resolved, child neglect ceased to be an issue and, in fact, this family became once more self-supporting.

Of course, in all of this it is well to bear in mind that the emotional part of the treatment takes place side by side with practical help. Let us reemphasize, therefore, how indecisive and immobilized many depressed mothers are when we first reach them. When a woman is in that state, it is often necessary to take hold of her life, kindly but gently making necessary decisions and carrying her along through necessary actions. Intervention by a relative may help. In a deep depression, psychiatric care will be indicated. But the mother will not be able to make up her mind to seek help in the first place, or choose where to go for it as her next step. In such a case, it is sometimes useful to point out to her that her inability to make up her mind is itself one of her symptoms—and what she must do to feel better. A depressed person with a history of good functioning most of her life has an excellent chance of improvement, given reasonably competent professional help. In persuading such a woman to take steps for herself (and her children), we can afford to be optimistic in our approach.

The Psychotic Mother

We come now to the last group of women whose neglect of their children stems from serious defects in their personalities. These are women who have one or another form of the serious mental disturbance referred to as psychosis. They are "out of contact with reality." Naturally a woman who is barely able to keep herself in touch with what is going on around her, who lives in a constant state of anger and fearfulness, a woman like this is in a poor position to offer her children competent mothering. There is a surprising number of such mothers. Not hospitalized, usually not so ill that they could be committed involuntarily, they are referred to as "ambulatory psychotics." Although it is true of only a minority, some psychotics are dangerous to their children, to themselves, and perhaps to their workers.

What Is Psychosis?

There are a number of kinds of psychosis. Two major groupings are disorders of thought and disorders of mood. In the mood disorders, depressions are extreme, or persons are constantly exhilarated and euphoric. In cases of thought disorders, there are confusion, incoherence, inability to follow a train of logic. Related to these symptoms is a loss of what is called "reality testing."

The key to a diagnosis of psychosis is whether there has been noteworthy loss of reality testing. When a person hears something or sees something that isn't there, he is hallucinating. This is a gross form of loss of reality testing. We also find delusional systems, as for example in the case of the isolated woman in a hill county who believes there is a worldwide conspiracy directed against her. Obviously in such people the ability to distinguish between what one is fantasying and what is really "out there" has been seriously damaged. Seldom, however, is reality testing completely gone in an ambulatory psychotic. Despite delusions, they often retain a good bit of practical sense that permits their moving around in the real world.

The diagnosis of psychosis takes specialized training and is best left to a psychiatrist if one is available. It would be inappropriate to encourage child welfare workers to attempt this judgment. It is necessary, however, to be alert to the possibility that the neglectful mother with whom one is dealing might be psychotic, in order that one can seek expert consultation or take whatever action seems indicated. Here are some symptoms that occur frequently, and that it is well to bear in mind:

1. *Social withdrawal.* This may show itself in marked shyness when around people, efforts to avoid social situations, or, in an extreme, staying by oneself all the time, like the mother who refuses to leave her bedroom.
2. *Loss of contact.* We see this, while interviewing, in the woman who seems unaware of what is going on around her, who drifts in and out of focus in her conversation, who seems at times to be staring aimlessly at a point far out in space. There is also the client who dashes around in disorganized fashion while with you. Silence is not the only expression of being out of contact, living in daydreams.
3. *Inappropriateness of mood.* One version of this is called "lability," in which mood veers wildly from sadness to hilarity and back again, as with a perpetual adolescent. Another form is shown by the person who laughs in the midst of discussing something painful, or smiles vacantly in the face of bad news. Perhaps most frequent, however, is the patient whose mood is inappropriate because it never seems to change. It ranges from dull apathy to torpid stolidity. This is also called "flatness of affect."
4. *Bizarre behaviors and grimaces.* Sometimes the client will talk to herself, laugh at nothing at all—unless she is responding to inner voices! Strange movements with arms, legs, facial contortions and the like are worth noting.
5. *Disturbances in the stream of thought.* It is useful to note whether the client talks gibberish. Coining new words or using malapropisms is sometimes indicative that a person heretofore intact is breaking down. Some persons also show an inability to break off a stream of speech, repeating the same thing over and over like a record that is stuck; related to this may be a need to mimic everything they hear.
6. *Delusional systems.* These are sometimes hard to discern. Some of the distortions of reality are relatively mild. That is, we know that something is wrong, but is it wrong enough to indicate psychosis? A woman absolutely refused to have her son vaccinated so he could enter school.

She was convinced that if he were vaccinated he would die. Forty or 50 years ago this belief was not uncommon among fearful mothers. But what does it mean now?

7. *Hallucinations.* Many clients are wise enough to refuse to admit having such symptoms except under highly skillful questioning. Therefore, we often infer the presence of hallucinations from bizarre reactions of the sort mentioned under point 4. The presence of hallucinations is ominous, of course.

8. *Severe anxiety*—a kind of formless, chronic state of terror. Not all psychotics experience this, but most do. It is not true that psychotics as a rule have no insight and are unaware there is anything wrong with them. A great many can feel themselves losing contact; they regard their own symptoms as strange and frightening. Anxiety is both the cause and the effect of this illness. It shows itself in myriad ways.

As noted, it is not the job of the soical worker to make a positive diagnosis. However, if he finds two or three of the foregoing features in combination, the client probably should also be seen by a psychiatrist.

The most common psychosis is schizophrenia. Its hallmarks are thought disorder, loss of reality testing and flatness of mood. One is also likely to see a person in a very severe depression, or as is said, "depressed to a psychotic degree"—disorganization and thought disorder, along with sadness and irritability. One characteristic of psychotic depression and of related manic states is the tendency for them to recur.

Finally, there is the person referred to as the borderline psychotic. Such a woman may show elements of various major psychiatric entities. At times she seems normal; at other times she may seem neurotic, psychotic, or to present a character disorder. It is hard to identify her because her fluctuating behavior is misleading. Only over a period of time, as we experience her relationship with us and observe her operate in the community, does a pattern emerge.

Mrs. Dawn is 35 years old, separated mother of four. The older children generally stay with the father, the youngest child, with her mother. Mrs. Dawn is neat and clean in appearance and wears appropriate clothing. However, she uses too much makeup, dyes her hair a different color frequently, and looks garish or "brassy."

Mrs. Dawn applied for AFDC because her husband "deserted" her. She has never had a permanent or definite abode. She moves two or three times a year, making her home with relatives of friends until she has a spat with them and moves on. Wherever she lives she keeps the place and the children neat and clean, sometimes under very adverse conditions.

When she first became known to the agency, Mrs. Dawn was suffering from high blood pressure and was hospitalized for a circulatory disorder. Later she complained of being unable to sleep. She paced the floor constantly and expressed fear that her husband or family might break in and kill her. She reported that her husband had been begging to see her and had been sleeping in a shed behind the house. Mrs. Dawn called the police. When they arrived, "he scampered off."

At one point Mrs. Dawn issued warrants for her husband's arrest for nonsupport. Mr. Dawn visited his wife and begged her to take up the warrants, showing her a doctor's statement that he was unable to work. A quarrel ensued when he refused to let her have the statement. Mrs. Dawn shot him in the leg with her gun and burned the doctor's paper. She then called the police to have him arrested for nonsupport. He did not press charges against her for shooting him, and he was imprisoned. A few months later Mrs. Dawn had a fight with her father and sister. She scratched them so badly they required medical attention. Mrs. Dawn accused her father and sister of stealing her money, and threatening to send her to a mental hospital.

Mrs. Dawn has always been able to present herself, on superficial contact, as a well-organized person. She was adept at enlisting the sympathy and help of lawyers and other community people to intervene on her behalf in her battles with welfare, her husband, landlords, etc.

After their fight, her father was persuaded to sign a warrant for her commitment. Mrs. Dawn ran frantically, hiding when anyone approached. A report was received that she was trying to buy guns so that she could shoot the caseworker and the sheriff. One night she was cornered in her house by the sheriff, who sent for the welfare director to help take her to the hospital. The welfare director was hit on the head with a pop bottle. But they got her to a mental hospital in the area.

The Dawn children were taken by Mrs. Dawn's parents. Later their father was released from prison. He took the children with him to another community where he had found employment.

At the mental hospital, authorities said they could not legally keep Mrs. Dawn beyond her emergency commitment because they did not have enough evidence from psychiatric examination to prove that she was psychotic. Mrs. Dawn requested discharge, and it was granted after 20 days in the hospital. Needless to say, the sheriff, the agency director and the caseworker were upset.

Mrs. Dawn began a long court battle for her children. The 4-year-old daughter was returned, but Mr. Dawn continues to keep the three boys. Mrs. Dawn seems to have given up. She has taken up residence with a man who she says is her cousin. Like her husband, he sometimes beats her.

Since her release from the hospital, Mrs. Dawn shows more psychotic features and is probably a borderline psychotic. Her affect is often inappropriate—she giggles suddenly for no reason. While telling of her boyfriend's violence, she begins to laugh uncontrollably. Her thinking is disordered—she starts a sentence and finishes with the ending of another sentence irrelevant to the first. Her associations are loose. She continues to be extremely manipulative. She associates with several other paranoid persons in town and, together, they stir up sympathy for themselves and hostility toward the agencies that must deal with them.

It is the opinion of some psychiatrists that the borderline patient represents a clinical entity bordering on normality, neurosis, psychosis and psychopathy, containing elements of any or all of these. In fact, many now believe that the patient remains more or less at the same level throughout her life—stable in her instability.

Over the years, the borderline patient has been given a number of other designations—preschizophrenia, pseudoneurotic psychotic, and the like. These terms indicate the sense that under a shaky adjustment on the surface lies severe disturbance. Although she lacks the grosser symptoms such as hallucinations, delusions or far-reaching disorganization, and we do not find typically wild mood swings, there is an absence of normal feelings, an extreme underlying mistrust of others, much barely concealed anger and meanness, and invariably, confusion about her identity—her role in life.

One of the characteristic features of borderline patients is that, when hospitalized, they rapidly pull themselves back together, and seem to be, at worse, severely neurotic. If this pattern is not recognized, planning for the children will be greatly complicated, as with Mrs. Dawn.

Effects on the Children

When the mother is in an acute psychosis, the obvious and immediate danger is the safety of her child. From time to time, we read in the papers of a woman who has killed her children and then herself. Of course, most such mothers are psychotic. Fortunately, such things happen rarely. Usually, the psychotic mother is merely an example of the woman who has no idea her child is being neglected. Lost in her fantasies, she may forget for hours at a time to feed the children; she may use very bad judgment about keeping them up late while she pursues a man or a feud, or about exposing them to scenes of violence. That a child's personality can be damaged by such experiences and by identification with a psychotic parent is obvious.

Treatment

Treating a psychotic person in order to restore her to reasonably constructive functioning, with minimal chances of further breakdown, is a job for the most highly skilled therapist. It cannot be attempted under the conditions of child welfare work. Our task, rather, is to learn to recognize the illness when it exists in our client, and handle her in terms of it.

Often this will require that her children be removed. But sometimes this cannot be arranged and sometimes it is not absolutely necessary. Therefore, the aim is to help the woman to be the best mother she can despite her illness. Following are some suggestions.

A cardinal rule in working with the psychotic mother is not to become involved in exploring her hidden fantasies or in making guesses about her unconscious motives. There is danger that interpreting motives of which she is not already aware will lead to further deterioration or a break-down. Many such women have a need to carry on tirades, so the worker will have to think through his policy in dealing with them. It is all right to listen sympathetically, at least for a time; it is often definitely not appropriate to argue with her or try to show her where she is wrong. But neither must one support her delusions. When she demands, "Don't you agree?", one can answer, "Well, I certainly know this is how *you* feel, because you've just been telling me." In other words, in dealing with an argumentative person, one can remain sympathetic while steadfastly refusing to join in her distortions.

As much as possible, the caseworker's task is to focus on issues that are current, concrete and need to be solved. One avoids generalities and symbolism in favor of, "How do you suppose we can get him ready for school on time?" There are two reasons for this approach. The first is to help this mother retain and strengthen her capacities for dealing with her real life, right now. Even more crucial, however, is the protection of her children. In the drama and excitement a psychotic mother can stir around her, it is possible to be diverted from this fundamental child welfare interest.

Bibliography

Borgman, Robert B. "Intelligence and Maternal Inadequacy." *Child Welfare*, 48 (1969), pp. 301-304.

Bowlby, John. "Grief and Mourning in Infancy and Early Childhood." *Psychoanalytic Study of the Child, Vol. XV*. New York: Basic Books, 1960.

Brison, David, W. "Definition, Diagnosis and Classification," in Alfred A. Baumeister, ed., *Mental Retardation*. Chicago: Aldine, 1967.

Lindemann, Erich, "Symptomatology and Management of Acute Grief," in Howard J. Parad, ed., *Crisis Intervention: Selected Readings*. New York: Family Service Association of America, 1965.

Pavenstedt, Eleanor, ed., *The Drifters: Children of Disorganized Lower-Class Families*. Boston: Little, Brown, 1967.

Polansky, Norman A., Borgman, Robert D., DeSaix, Christine, and Smith, Betty Jane. "Two Modes of Maternal Immaturity and Their Consequences." *Child Welfare*, 49 (1970), pp. 312-323.

Polansky, Norman A., DeSaix, Christine, Wing, Mary Lou, and Patton, John D. "Child Neglect in a Rural Community." *Social Casework*, 49 (1968), pp. 467-475.

Prevalent Types of Neglectful Mothers

Redlich, Fredrick C., and Freedman, Daniel X. *The Theory and Practice of Psychiatry*. New York: Basic Books, 1966.

Sarason, Seymour B. "Mental Subnormality," in Redlich and Freedman, *op. cit.*

CHAPTER FIVE

Processes of Treatment

In discussing the types of neglectful mothers, we have already begun to offer suggestions about casework approaches. Therefore, it must be clear by now that it is no more possible to speak of *the* treatment of child neglect than it is of *the* neglectful mother. It is impossible to compress here all that a worker should know about handling these difficult cases. It takes years of learning and practice to acquire skill and sureness. We confine this discussion to generalities about casework that need especially to be borne in mind in treating child neglect; and go into detail only about some matters of technique that are widely applicable in dealing with infantile women, but that we have not found to be universally known.

What Is Treatment?

The aim of casework treatment is to bring about more or less permanent change in the client in what seems to be a desirable direction. The process is one in which the worker intends to make himself unnecessary, and may succeed in doing so. Many of us have the feeling we are not "doing anything" unless we are delivering concrete services, such as bringing food or moving a child or getting a family into better housing. These actions may well be part of a process of bringing about change, and they may be essential first-aid measures. However, in many cases important phases of treatment occur just by sitting and talking. In short, there is no single royal road to casework; treatment is not one technique or one set of actions.

In instances of child neglect, the most reliable alteration occurs when we have helped the mother become a more adequate, less infantile person. Or, we can try to alter the mother's life circumstances so that, although she is not much different than she was before, she does care for her children at a much better level. The danger then is that if she does not get continuing support, she may slip backward.

Rarely does an immature client sustain progress and growth without backsliding from time to time. What seems improvement may be just a shift in symptoms. One must expect no miracles, but look forward to treating the neglectful mother through good times and bad until gains are well consolidated, and she has functioned on a good level for months. Because of the unevenness of movement in clients, and their typical lapses from grace, it is expectable that one will feel discouragement repeatedly with each neglectful mother. At such times, it is important that the worker, too, have someone to whom he can turn for support. Hopefully, this will be a supervisor with longer-range perspective on the case, who is able to remind the worker that "futility is contagious." But, if the agency situation does not already provide this support—who supervises the supervisor?—one may have to arrange it.[1]

Making the Initial Contact

The first, and certainly a natural, question asked by caseworkers is, "How can we get in?" In most cases one enters the home uninvited and not even understood. Forming a relationship depends on a worker who has strong convictions about the needs of children, and no great need to be popular with everyone she meets.

Concerning conviction about the worker's role, we can only repeat that child neglect is a serious thing, leading to immediate or long-range danger to the children in the family. When we get the sordid details of charges brought by informants, we do not know if they are true, and we give the mother the benefit of the doubt. It does happen that complaints are filed maliciously and a mother's misbehavior is exaggerated. But it is more often true that the informant has reached a decision to report a family only after he could no longer withstand the proddings of his conscience. We take it for granted that the welfare worker has both a duty and a right to investigate a complaint, whether from the community or from some official agency such as the school, the court or the police.

There are some rules of thumb about the mechanics for making an initial contact. For example, any client deserves the courtesy of prearranging an initial appointment, with an opportunity to change the time if it is inconvenient to her. Only in situations that strike us as emergencies, or after we have found our more courteous approach a failure, do we literally "barge in."

If the worker is expected, he can usually be pretty sure the mother will be more afraid of him than he is of her. The mother will be anxious; she may also be depressed, angry, humiliated, bewildered, relieved—or any combination of these. And she may well express these feelings through withdrawal, denial, an attitude that the best defense is to attack, or a show of feigned friendliness and pseudoacquiescence. In the latter case, it just means she is saving her resentment for later.

Although the children are uppermost in the worker's mind, he will do well to concentrate on the person he is encountering. His display of concern should be for the mother first, and her children second. In this way, her own needs to be special may be met. The tone of the visit may also be softened so that it is not seen as a flaunting of authority, which may well be a factor in the background, or a deliberate intrusion, but a sincere offer to help. "We have been told there are some problems here, and it is our job to look into such things and help parents in all matters concerning their children." This is tactful, but is actually also a strong and flexible position from which to operate.

Very often the mother will divert her anger from the worker and lash out at the complainant. With this one does not argue, of course, since it may clear the air for the moment for her to get such feelings out. Nonetheless, one should soon try to get communication opened up. "Do you also feel angry because you think *I* am prying?" "Do you feel we are butting into things that are none of our business?" It does not hurt to let the mother save face by expressing her resentment. It is not so necessary to answer an attack as to hear it out. The aim is not to win an argument with her about whether she has a right to be angry, but to win a relationship for the sake of the children. Strength and calmness in the face of attack, even if directly at the worker, usually has a settling effect, and increases her respect for one. If one asks how these characteristics are acquired, we can only reply, "The more you do it, the easier it becomes." For after a time, an experienced child welfare worker handles anger like an electrician deals with current. We respect its force and potential for danger, but we are not all that frightened when we believe we know what we are doing.

A final practical hint is this: When dealing with a childlike and manipulative person, it is well not to take her more seriously than she takes herself.

itical Decisions

Important to the role of the worker in treating child neglect is, of course, the exercise of judgment. We cannot afford to delay, hoping against hope that something will turn up. It is well to remember that to take no action is also a decision.

The courses open to us are limited:

. . . We can decide to go away, concluding that the complaint did not have enough substance to justify action.

. . . We can decide that the mother involved is untreatable, or at least there is no one present in the area who can treat her, and try to have the children permanently removed.

. . . .We may feel that the mother might be treatable, but the only way to test this is to make a trial of it; meanwhile, we will avoid complications by leaving the children with her.

. . . We may think that she is treatable, but will improve, if at all, only after a long time; therefore, despite the fact that the family is not hopeless, the children should be removed for the present.

. . . We can remove the children as a way to increase parental motivation to change themselves and their situation, holding out return of the children as an inducement to cooperate in treatment.

There are some permutations on these, but basically these are the alternatives open to us in making recommendations, and to the judge in making his decision. We often cannot do what would be ideal, but we have a professional responsibility to decide what an ideal solution would be, and come as close to it as we are able.

The Use of Authority

Much has been written about the use of legal authority in dealing with neglectful mothers. The caseworker is helped to accept the unaccustomed position of representing the law and the potential use of force. Yet to be a representative of legal authority is not all bad from the standpoint of treatment. The fact that he represents a potential threat can add to respect for the worker. Whether it interferes with his ability to talk sympathetically with the neglectful mother depends a great deal on how comfortable he is about having some legal power at his disposal. One can say, "If you are not able to do anything about the way things are for the kids, I will be obliged to get them the help they need until you can." Although the mother may feel called upon to protest, she often greets the announcement with relief. After all, someone has finally come along who has both the concern and the power to take control of what she herself recognizes to be a deteriorating mess in her household.

Child neglect, in short, almost always expresses chaos within the parents. Although they may protest mightily against us, they also find reassurance in the idea than an outside person is about to do what they have not had the inner strength to do—impose order in their lives.

Fostering Dependency

Nearly all public welfare departments have policies directing their staffs to avoid actions that foster dependency. The fear is that people will learn to look to the agency for financial support they might otherwise earn. The social work profession as a whole has strong values against creating "dependent" relationships between the worker and his clients. Such a relationship is felt to be demeaning and potentially harmful, since it is thought to undermine self-determination and other evidences of maturity.

Nevertheless, we next undertake something in seeming contradiction to these well-accepted values. We provide a set of approaches and techniques by which the worker may deliberately encourage an immature, neglectful mother to form a dependent tie to him. Why do we do this? We do it in part because words play peculiar tricks in our field. Although the many forms of dependency are related, they are by no means identical.

It is simply not true that one should never foster dependency. Many infantile mothers can relate at first only in a dependent way. We do not create their dependency; they are already dependent. The only question is: To whom will they attach themselves? Unless the worker enters their lives through this means he runs the risk of leaving himself no treatment leverage at all. A disorganized, deprived mother may have to live through a stage in which she lets herself be dependent while she grows and gains strength to the point where she no longer needs help. The refusal of the agency or inability of a worker to accept the client's emotional dependency may prolong her financial dependency, as illustrated by the Hall case:

> The AFDC record described Mrs. Hall as a small, attractive woman in her mid-30s with four children ranging in ages from 6 to 16. She applied for assistance when she separated from Mr. Hall because of his cruelty. Following a court hearing in which he was ordered to make support payments, he disappeared. For years Mrs. Hall and the agency exerted their energies in trying to locate him. He telephoned from time to time from some unknown place saying that if she dropped the warrants, he would return and help her. She has stubbornly refused, saying she would rather see him in prison, and she has been supported by the agency in her stand.

> When Mrs. Hall was 3 years old, her own parents were separated, and her father placed her and her elder sister, the only children, in an orphanage. Throughout the years, Mrs. Hall leaned on her sister and her father. When she and Mr. Hall separated, she tried to live with her father and his second wife, but they could not have her or did not want her. Her sister, by turn, one time welcomes her dependency and another time rejects her.

> Being helpless and appealing, Mrs. Hall aroused the interest of a group in the community. She worked hard in an unskilled job and received some supplementation from AFDC. The women of her church took on her and her problems as "a project." They found an attractive house, furnished it, and even gave a linen shower for Mrs. Hall. They usurped the agency responsibility, and Mrs. Hall naturally turned to them and against the caseworker. She became demanding on the church group so that, after 2 months, they dropped her. She had no one to help her with the rent,

59

which was too high for AFDC, and no friends to lean on. She had to move and turned to her oldest daughter to cling to.

Then illness struck. Mrs. Hall was hospitalized, and the public agency moved in with full AFDC, a homemaker, and day care services for the younger children. When Mrs. Hall was discharged she returned to work. Immediately, AFDC was discontinued, the homemaker was removed, and the children were taken from day care—the agency wanted "to encourage Mrs. Hall's independence." For several months the family bumped along on an inadequate income from low-paying employment, complicated by unreliable babysitters, frequent illness of the children, medical bills and Mrs. Hall's own poor health.

Finally, it was necessary for the public agency to help again. The oldest child was upset and doing poorly in school. The psychologist found her old beyond her years, sharing the responsibility of the mother's dependency and care of the younger children.

A homemaker was assigned and the children were again placed in day care. In the following months considerable progress was seen in the family; Mrs. Hall could work regularly, and she regained confidence in herself. More important, the homemaker, an efficient, motherly type of woman, became Mrs. Hall's confidant, and was strong enough to be leaned upon. This meant that Mrs. Hall did not need to use her daughter so much, and the child's school adjustment improved. In fact, things were going so well that the caseworker seldom visited the family, and it was not long until the agency again felt that Mrs. Hall should be independent, and removed the homemaker.

From the time of her first hospitalization, Mrs. Hall had complained about her health. Almost immediately after the homemaker left and independence was forced upon her, she required hospitalization and a hysterectomy was performed. AFDC was reinstated. When his mother went to the hospital, the youngest child refused to go to school. In psychological testing he was found to feel rejected and unloved by his mother. He had always stirred up trouble to get her attention, and he thought she had deserted him by going to the hospital. When she came home, Mrs. Hall became depressed and became completely dependent on her oldest child. She developed anger and hostility toward the doctors who were treating her but who could find no basis for her continued complaints. She accused them of not caring for her because she was a welfare recipient.

At about this time, a new caseworker was assigned. He seemed to recognize Mrs. Hall's dependency. The worker began to visit twice each week and arranged for a telephone to be installed so that Mrs. Hall could telephone when she wanted to talk with him. Mrs. Hall began to pour out her long-pent-up hostility toward Mr. Hall and repeated over and over again incidents of abuse and neglect. She felt that she had also been deserted by her father, her mother and her sister. She needed almost constant encouragement and support from the caseworker, who had taken on more than usual responsibility in the family; the worker shopped for them or took the oldest child to do the shopping; the school called for him when one of the children needed help or transportation; he saw that they had proper medical and dental care.

Mrs. Hall developed symptoms that might have explained her complaints. Despite her anger with the medical profession, Mrs. Hall was persuaded by the caseworker to choose and go to a doctor. It was found that she had a tumor that required surgery. She also needed treatment for chronic infection. Dental care was planned because her teeth were the suspected cause of the infection.

Gradually, Mrs. Hall began to improve and was talking of going to work. At this point the agency again decided that Mrs. Hall must become independent, and the caseworker was advised in supervision to cut his visits and services. When the worker tried to explain the new relationship to Mrs. Hall, she refused to talk to him. She became withdrawn and detached. Her conversation consisted of giving only factual information necessary to the continuing of AFDC. The worker, on his monthly visits, continued to express understanding of her anger with doctors, her family, and now with him. He sympathized with her discomforts, and he took her thoughtful small gifts—magazines, curlers for her hair.

With this turn of events, the oldest child decided that she would quit school to care for her mother, who had again turned to her. The worker was able to salvage his relationship with the girl, expressing understanding that she had replaced him with her mother and interpreting to her some of her mother's real need—someone she could lean on, not someone to stay with her constantly. He arranged for the girl to have good new clothes for entering her senior year of high school.

The caseworker recognized that the relationship was severed too quickly and regretted not being able to "taper off," during which time he could have helped Mrs. Hall to greater independence through a transitional period of mutual understanding.

The pattern of being "dropped" started when Mrs. Hall was 3 years old. "Her parents were separated and she was left with her father who placed her and her sister in an orphanage." She felt deserted by both parents and she married a man on whom she could not depend. Her emotional needs had never been met. Throughout her life, she pushed herself into dependency relationships that always have resulted in her being deserted, and her children suffered the consequence. Mrs. Hall demonstrated her ability to manage and reach for independence through dependency relationships, but none of them lasted long enough or were handled so that she could herself mature.

There are, then, immature, often self-preoccupied mothers who must be reached at first by encouraging a childlike, dependent tie. How does the caseworker bring this about? This is asking how we can do deliberately something we often do unconsciously, and then may have to undo! In any case, here are some suggestions:

1. *Frequent contacts.* As a general rule, the more frequently two people are in contact with each other, the more meaningful they become to each other. Since infantile people form dependent ties when they get attached, the more frequently they are seen, the greater the dependency. However, especially at first, long interviews are not indicated. Most of these women do not have all that much to talk about, and they become uneasy about socializing before they are ready. Therefore, we lean toward what our colleague, Donald Boone, describes as "many shallow contacts." One makes opportunities to stop by en route to someplace else, to drop off a message or pick up a form or the like. The same holds for welcoming drop-ins at the worker's office—for 5 to 15 minutes or so. (Geographical districting facilitates this.) This also helps to counter the intense loneliness that afflicts immature women.

2. *Concrete giving.* After the foregoing it hardly seems necessary to note that a great many of the neglectful mothers want to be given to, and will respond at first only on the basis of, "What's there in it for me." Such concrete examples of caring as transportation to a medical clinic, financial assistance when justified, interceding with a landlord, and so forth, are real and understandable to the woman operating at a more primitive level. We all resist relief in kind nowadays, but workers who do well with child neglect include those who personally bring their clients clothes and furnishings they have discovered are needed. Nearly all successful workers agree that in the initial phases of treatment they do a great many things *for* the client, before she becomes able to do them *with* them. Thus, the worker simultaneously protects the children and elicits dependency.

3. *Feeding the need to be special.* There remains enough of the child in any one of us that we react gratefully to evidence that we are being singled out and have a special stature in another's eyes. There are a number of ways the caseworker can do this. When he is talking with the client in his office, for example, he should resist interruptions, and make a point that he is resisting them. He can also feed this need by focusing his attention sharply on the mother—not only by watching and listening closely, but by showing his awareness of her current feelings.

4. *Demeanor.* The initial impression the worker makes is very important in dealing with immature clients. Any of us would rather attach himself to a warm, thoughtful, giving person who is also strong. The cues used by neglectful mothers in forming judgments may seem superficial, but they have to be taken into account. A ready smile, a nonhostile manner, a soft and pleasant voice make a difference. The preferred style of speech is

deliberate, easily understood. It is all right to show one is troubled, at times, but being flustered by trivia is not reassuring. One need not claim to know everything, but it may be frightening to a client who is growing dependent on a worker if the worker seems helpless. Why not, "I'll have to find out about that," rather than, "Gosh, that's something I don't know anything about."

5. *Tact.* Social workers may confuse tact with indirection and gingerliness. Tact simply implies sensitivity to the other person's feelings, and a willingness not to make her feel bad when it can be avoided. Exaggerated tact may be interpreted as weakness, which will tend to rupture a dependent tie.

6. *Discussing feelings.* Dependency is also increased by the worker's interest in his client's feelings. In fact, as with frequency of contact, the more that feelings can be aired, the more likely that a tie will be established. (We have more to say about this in the next section on Verbal Accessibility.)

7. *Minimal demandingness.* Part of being infantile is to be selfish, and it will be some time before the typical neglectful mother cares enough about her worker to make any effort on the worker's behalf, or even distinguishes him as a fellow human being. Premature demands on a client, especially if they require her to attempt something that is hard for her to do, destroy the evolving dependency relationship. They also display insensitivity.

8. *Moral insulation.* Workers successful with neglectful mothers are relatively shock-proof. This does not mean they have no standards; but it does mean they are sufficiently sophisticated so that they are not aghast at things the mother has done, or feelings she displays. Her emotions and impulses are likely to be raw and direct, as with any child. When hurt, she wants revenge; she knows little pity. Her sex life is often as chaotic as her child rearing. Therefore, she is put off by someone whose reactions strike her as squeamish or namby-pamby. She sees moralizing as weakness and as a rejection of what she is.

Our greatest need for these techniques in treating child neglect is in strengthening the initial bond between client and worker. For unless the worker has something the client wants, there will be no reason for her to want to stay in touch with him, and certainly no reason she should try to please him. This is what we mean by initial treatment leverage. A second reason for fostering dependency is the number of neglectful mothers we see who are lonely and terribly deprived people. In moving to "feed their dependency," we give them some reassurance that the world is a safer place than they believed. We also provide for them a model they may conceivably emulate in meeting their children's needs, in turn. An unspoken part of any casework is offering ourselves as persons with whom the client may wish to identify.

Meeting dependency is a phase of treatment that may have to last for a long time, much longer than most agencies seem to recognize. A woman who never had the loving all youngsters deserve during the first 5 years of her life is not going to make up for it in eight lively contacts with a busy child welfare worker. She may never make up for it, but her emptiness may in time be partly assuaged. At a minimum our concern reassures her on one crucial point. She is not an unlovable person. This is the most dreadful anxiety of all.

After a time, we shall want to diminish the dependency. In doing it, we gently but steadily reverse the flow we have described. Visiting is spaced out to longer intervals; we are not so readily available as before, and may mention that others' needs are also pressing. We decline to make decisions of which the client is capable, and we make more realistic requirements of her, such as waiting between visits or coming to see us. "Can you come into the office next Monday around 3?" "Oh, I think you are able to handle this yourself very well now."

We focus less of our talk around her feelings and more on discussion of practical arrangements in her life. We may now begin to challenge distorted statements when she makes them. We make ourselves emotionally unnecessary, leaving her freed, we hope, to attach herself to others who will be more continually in her life, such as her family, her husband and children, her friends. As we do this, we often have to handle our own need to be needed. Detachment from a well-loved client will leave an empty place in our lives, too.

Promoting Verbal Accessibility

In Chapter Two we mentioned the usefulness of watching the client's Verbal Accessibility in arriving at a tentative psychodiagnosis. Verbal Accessibility (or VA) is defined as the readiness of the client to talk about her most important feelings and attitudes, and to permit discussion of these with her caseworker. We have found VA to be a surprisingly reliable and economical measure in assessing the current maturity of a woman's functioning and in judging her prognosis for treatment.

To appraise Verbal Accessibility requires no special procedures. The only tool needed is the acuteness of the worker who makes himself alert to what is being said, and not said, by his client. One scale for judging it was given in Chapter Two. Another more detailed method is set forth in Appendix B.

Inaccessibility may stem from intellectual limitations that are unchangeable after a person is an adult. In most cases, however, it indicates less personal maturity in the mother. In general, people who are more competent are more likely to feel they can control their behavior; therefore, they need not be so afraid to know their feelings. We found that, as a general rule, the mother who was well able to discuss feelings with her worker was likely to be meeting the basic needs of her children. This is not a 100% correspondence, but it is a rather dependable rule. Mothers who were verbally inaccessible were also more afflicted with feelings of deep loneliness. They had never formed strong social relationships nor had typical social experiences in adolescence. They achieved less in school, had limited dating before marriage, and were unlikely to have held employment outside the home.

One might throw up his hands and say the inaccessible client is untreatable, and let things go at that. However, this is like a doctor saying he will refuse to set a man's broken leg because he does not bring himself to the office. In other words, we need to make an effort to raise the client's VA in order to ready her for treatment. Promoting the client's VA goes further than that, for we have reason to believe that as the mother becomes more accessible in interviews she is also maturing and getting better. When the Apathetic-Futile woman becomes angry with her worker, and can open up about her hostility and put it into words, this is a sign that she is already moving toward health, for what has been buried within her is now coming out and she is taking responsibility for it. The Impulse-Ridden mother is much, much safer when she is talking about her emotions rather than expressing them with her behavior and, indeed, her whole life. We have stressed the role of ventilation in lifting a depression. For all these reasons, we believe that the treatment of many mothers involved in child neglect does well to concentrate on promoting their Verbal Accessibility. Indeed, this is the treatment of choice.

Because of the caseworker's importance in so many cases, we have made a study of how average workers react to the nonverbal mother, how they handle this technical problem. We found that the typical worker has no plan, and does not handle it; rather, he is handled by the client's symptom. The noncommunicative mother generates frustration and feelings of rejection. First, the worker becomes impatient; then he tries to reach her through concrete services and making suggestions (which go unheeded); finally, he finds reasons to leave her alone. If keeping her distance from the worker is the intent of this maneuver on the mother's part, it certainly succeeds.

The woman in greatest need of help is typically minded to be concrete. Her concerns are food, clothing and shelter for herself and her children. She is chronically lonely and clings to her children and her husband because these are the only sources of human warmth she expects to have. She is extremely hesitant to chance attaching herself to a caseworker who, as she sees it, may abandon her at any time. Moreover, so far as she is concerned, talking has never solved a problem in her life. An additional handicap is her restricted vocabulary. If she were aware of nuances in her feelings, she would be at a loss to find words for them.

Here is a set of guidelines for heightening VA, chosen for relevance to working with the mother involved in marginal child caring. We state these principles simply, but of course some of them have implications that are not simple at all.

1. *The first necessity is a willingness to talk.* Not all verbalizing is indicative of verbal accessibility. One may use rapid speech in order to avoid speaking about what matters most. This mechanism is also found among neglectful mothers. After having been drowned in a long, circumstantial tale of woes with the kitchen stove, the worker may emerge knowing no more about what the mother thinks about anything of importance than he did before. Still, we have found that women who will talk at all are more likely to become truly accessible eventually. The first step, therefore, may be to encourage conversation with such a client, no matter the topic. If she will open up about crops or cucumbers or the best road to town, that is enough to start with.

2. *Begin with the concrete, external and superficial.* Many of these women are minded to be concrete, and this fact must be taken into account in dealing with them. To "explain the policy to Mrs. B" is useless. Mrs. B often cannot grasp the reasons for agency policy; it will be enough if she can learn what the policy is. Her acceptance of the policy has little to do with understanding it, anyway, and the attempt to make her understand is self-indulgence on the part of the worker.

From the discussion of external matters entree to feelings may be gained. Rebudgeting required to accommodate a daughter's illegitimate baby can lead to a flood of feelings of remorse and concern about the pregnancy—*if* the worker will listen to them.

3. *Security encourages expansiveness.* The lack of emotional support in the lives of many neglectful mothers is unbelievable. A number of such mothers have blossomed under the simple attention of our getting their life histories for research. In general, we find that support through improving the client's self-image is conducive to VA. If a woman raises succulent October beans, makes good biscuits or irons well, honest praise and a desire to learn from her are ways of conveying admiration. Freedom to talk about attitudes rises proportionately.

4. *Feelings have names.* It does not take much subtlety for a woman to say, "I could murder my husband," but it might shock her to blurt it out, and it probably indicates more violence than she really means. The lack of words like "irritated, provoked, sore" can handicap a woman from labeling feelings she would otherwise express. So she may say nothing. One service we can perform for the client trying to learn to describe important attitudes is to teach her verbal symbols that will help her say what she wants to. This may be especially important in a lower-class milieu in which the expression of nuances is not encouraged, and the common vocabulary is all too meager.

5. *Opportunities pass.* In our wish to comfort young workers that "all roads lead to Rome" and errors can be corrected, we may go too far. There is such a thing as wasting a chance to deepen the level of communication, a chance that may never recur. If the worker shrinks back or is unable to share the mother's grief in a moment of crisis, he heightens a barrier. If he cannot stand to talk about her anger toward the agency or toward himself, that does the same. Some opportunities are less dramatic, but still real, such as taking a mother to the clinic, spending 2 or 3 hours in the privacy of the moving auto without the hindrances to talking encountered when she is visited at home. Here is a chance for increasing one's knowledge of the mother, as well as offering her a needed service.

6. *Talk has a background and repercussions.* In some rural subcultures, for example, there is an injunction against discussing "family troubles" outside the home. In fact, they usually are not verbalized inside the home, either.[2] Hence, a woman who finds herself describing problems she may have had with her own mother or with a child is in effect violating her own culture. Similarly, we are all familiar with the guilt that follows an outburst against someone who is loved, so the woman who fills our office with recriminations in a first interview may never appear for a second.

The worker must be sensitive to these repercussions within the client who breaks through her inhibitions. He needs to take time for reassurance about these aftereffects before he ends the interview. Otherwise he will be met with greater resistance the next time. The mother may blame him for what she said, since he encouraged her to get it out. He should ask, "How do you think you are going to feel later about what you have been telling me?" Or even close with, "Well, you may get the feeling you have said some very angry things, but what you say is not all that bad—and, anyhow, saying it here won't hurt anybody."

A treatment setting that often counteracts cultural inhibitions against revealing feelings is the therapy group. The norm in the therapy group is to open up; members come to reward each other for doing so. A number of attempts to use group techniques with inadequate mothers are now under way throughout the country. This is a device well worth considering for those mothers self-confident enough to bring themselves to a group meeting when we first know them, or who can be encouraged to try the experience after some time in individual casework.

7. *Honesty is the only policy.* For a caseworker to talk about an AFDC mother's going to work while knowing well she has no present capacity for doing so, while the mother gives lip service to the same hypocrisy, is a mutually corrupting experience. It hardly bespeaks a relationship in which VA will flourish. Similarly, a worker who feels she must defend an irrational and meager food budget is hardly confirming an atmosphere of frank talk

about real attitudes. The same is true of false compliments, and evading the mother's shortcomings.

8. *How verbally accessible are you?* Finally, we come to the worker's own readiness to act both as listener and role model in helping the mother become more verbally accessible. We do not mean the worker must tell the mother all about himself in the hope of seducing her to do likewise. But, it is appropriate to share, from time to time, how one feels at the moment. It is our observation that those workers who have trouble talking about their own feelings are unlikely to be able to help marginal mothers "stand behind their words." To encourage another to discuss important attitudes, it is first necessary to be able to bear hearing them. And to bear another's angry, despairing — yes, and soft and loving — feelings, one must be comfortable with one's own.

Conclusion

We have set down the gist of what we have learned about helping mothers involved in child neglect or child care that is marginal. The learning is from research as well as from distilling our experiences as caseworkers and those of others we have known. It must be clear now that although many instances of child neglect can be solved only by rescuing and placing the children, a sizable proportion of the mothers are able to change and mature. A large proportion of all neglectful mothers are disorganized, infantile women. Although we make no bones about the difficulty of helping them, one must be neither cynical nor fatuous in assessing their chances.

In talking about treatment, we have stayed close to the real world in which the average child welfare worker operates. It is possible to conceive of other approaches to treatment not mentioned here, going as far as the use of a total institutional environment to facilitate change. The original intent of Maxwell Jones's "therapeutic community" was to treat persons similar to those described here. But in most cases such help is not available, and would not be practical even if it were.

The essence of the process of treatment of immature people is a willingness to get involved. We offer to entangle ourselves in their sometimes messy affairs in the confidence that together we shall find our ways into the clear. Involvement in neglected families makes great demands, of course. It means living with, or near, hostility, since these deprived women are so loaded with it. It requires meeting dependency needs. In fact, we may even encourage them—not to be dependent, for they are already that—to attach their dependency temporarily to us. Finally, involvement between adults requires movement toward increasing verbal honesty and directness on both sides if it is to reach toward growth.

It is commonplace when speaking of treating difficult cases to extol the

68

virtues of persistence. This is too polite a way to put it. Those workers who successfully treat infantile mothers are usually stubborn. One's stubbornness is often a nuisance in one's life. But child neglect is a social problem in which a worker's stubbornness can be harnessed to improving the lives of whole families. We recommend it.

References

1. Our observations here confirm those of Professor Mary Sullivan of the Jane Addams Graduate School of Social Work, University of Illinois, who has discussed her experience with us.

2. See David H. Looff, *Appalachia's Children: The Challenge of Mental Health.* Lexington, Ky.: University Press of Kentucky, 1971.

Bibliography

Garrett, Annette. *Interviewing: Its Principles and Methods.* New York: Family Service Association of America, 1942.

Hollis, Florence. *Casework: A Psychosocial Therapy.* New York: Random House, 1964.

Jones, Maxwell. *The Therapeutic Community.* New York: Basic Books, 1953.

Parad, Howard J., and Miller, Roger R., editors. *Ego-Oriented Casework: Problems and Perspectives.* New York: Family Service Association of America, 1963.

Polansky, Norman A. "Challenging Concepts of Social Work Treatment of the Multi-Problem Client," in *Changing Services for Changing Clients.* New York: National Association of Social Workers, 1969.

Polansky, Norman A. *Ego Psychology and Communication: Theory for the Interview.* Chicago: Aldine-Atherton, 1971.

Ruesch, Jurgen. *Therapeutic Communication.* New York: W. W. Norton & Co., 1961.

Appendix A

CHILDHOOD LEVEL OF LIVING SCALE

The Scale

The Childhood Level of Living Scale (CLL) was developed by the University of Georgia Child Research Field Station staff[1] to be used as an indicator of the conditions of care under which children are reared—in fact, to measure the child's "level of living." The scale follows somewhat the approach used by Sears *et al.,*[2] but, whereas they were concerned about whether mothers forced the children to eat, we were concerned about whether the mother offered any food at all. An important reason for pitching the scale at so low a level was to give the respondent a greater chance to be above the lowest level, with the better feeling, "Well, at least things aren't *that* bad in this household."

How to Use the Scale

Persons should be thoroughly familiar with the entire content and overall purpose of the CLL scale prior to attempting to use it. Although designed for "yes-no" answers, this is not basically a question-answer form. It is for the worker to complete—never the mother. Many of the questions are best answered through observation, while others ask for information best obtained from collateral sources such as teachers, welfare workers, public health workers, and so forth. It is not necessary to begin with Item 1 and continue consecutively through the other items. There are, however, certain groupings of items that lend themselves to completion during one interview.

The instrument is designed to be flexible. Items can be rephrased or expanded for clarity, if necessary, as long as the meaning remains unchanged. We would suggest that the Key to Scoring be covered or deleted in duplication when attempting to scale a family, so that the suggested direction does not influence the worker's judgment.

---

[1]Dr. Norman A. Polansky, Director, and staff members Miss Betty Jane Smith, Mrs. Mary Lou Wing, Mrs. Christine DeSaix, and Robert Borgman developed the scale.

[2]Robert R. Sears, Eleanor E. Maccaby, Harry Levin, *Patterns of Child Rearing* (New York: Harper and Row, 1957).

Scoring

The scale is so scored that a high score indicates problematic or actual low level of living. Conversely, the lower the score the better the level of living. Wherever a plus mark (+) appears, it is counted as 1 point. For scoring purposes items were grouped to make composite scores where all items were related to a specific area of child caring, (e.g., Hygiene). Total +s in any score or subscale should be counted, with the few exceptions indicated.

Definitions

The following definitions were used in making assessments:

A. Terms generally used
  1. Appears—is readily apparent from observation
  2. Complains—expresses discontent with the situation
  3. Expresses—reveals in any manner, as in words, gestures or actions
  4. Mentions—spontaneous reference to
  5. Plans—intentional ordering or arranging to achieve purpose or goal
  6. Routine—conforming to a habitual course of procedure
  7. Seems—apparent from observation
B. Relative to specific items
  1. Item 3—"naked dropcord"; no fixture, receptacle for bulb only
  2. Item 5—"potbellied stove"; if standard is lower, please note
  3. Item 11—"stovepipes to flue"; as contrasted with going directly through wall or roof, the latter being considered fire hazard
  4. Item 16—"dilapidated"; a house that does not provide safe and adequate shelter, and its condition endangers the health, safety or well-being of its occupants
  5. Items 24 and 25—"meal courses"; either meat and one vegetable or two vegetables
  6. Item 26—"special occasions"; birthdays, Thanksgiving, Christmas, etc.
  7. Item 39—"insufficiently older sibling"; child less than 12 years old or any person who could not reasonably be expected to provide adequate care
  8. Item 49—"other than doctors or nurses"; faith healer, voodoo, etc.
  9. Item 90—"educational toys"; puzzles, building blocks, modeling clay, etc.
  10. Item 126—"takes pride in"; expresses pleasure in, enjoyment from, or feeling of accomplishment concerning

Interpretation of Scoring

As an example of the application of this scale, the table that follows shows a quintile distribution of Childhood Level of Living scores based upon a

Childhood Level of Living Scale

sample consisting of 65 mother-child pairs living in western North Carolina. All families had a reported income below $3000 annually. Both of the child's parents were at least nominally in the home. These families included all those in the county who met our sample criteria, except perhaps a few who were either so geographically isolated or mobile that their children could not attend the Head Start program.

	Total Score	Physical Care	Emotional/ Cognitive Care
Severe Child Neglect	65-99	38-63	27-38
Child Neglect	49-64	27-37	21-26
Marginal Child Care	35-48	17-26	16-20
Minimal Child Neglect	21-34	7-16	11-15
No Indication of Child Neglect	7-21	1-6	3-10

Note: If the scale is to be used for research purposes, a Childhood Level of Living Scale Manual is available from Dr. Norman A. Polansky, School of Social Work, University of Georgia, Athens, Ga.

CHILDHOOD LEVEL OF LIVING SCALE
Items and Scoring
Part A — Physical Care

	Yes	No
I. Comfort		
1. Water is piped into the house		+
2. Hot water is piped to a faucet		+
3. Light bulbs are from naked dropcords	+	
4. The mother complains of difficulty in heating house	+	
5. One potbellied stove is only means of heating house other than cook stove	+	
6. The house is heated by coal or oil		+
7. Family lives mostly in one room in winter because of difficulty in heating entire house	+	
II. Safety		
8. There are at least two exits to the house		+
9. The exits are easily opened		+
10. Electrical wiring appears to be frayed or overloaded	+	
11. Stovepipes go directly to chimney or flue		+
12. Fires are sometimes started with kerosene or other inflammable agent	+	
III. State of Repair		
13. Repairs one usually makes oneself are left undone	+	
14. The roof of house leaks	+	
15. Windows have been cracked or broken over a month without repair	+	
16. House is dilapidated	+	
17. House is neither papered nor painted inside	+	
IV. Hygiene		
18. There is an inside toilet		+
19. There is an outside toilet	+	
20. There are window screens in good repair in most windows		+
21. There are screen doors properly mounted		+
X. Housing Composite (Combined scores of foregoing four scales)		

Key to Scoring

	Key to Scoring	
	Yes	No

V. Feeding Patterns

22. Child complains of being hungry to parent, teachers or others	+	
23. Mother plans for variety in foods		+
24. Mother plans at least one meal a day consisting of two courses		+
25. Mother plans meals with courses that go together		+
26. Mother plans special meals for special occasions		+
27. Child is offered food at fixed time each day		+
28. Mother expresses concern about feeding child balanced diet		+
29. Mother makes effort to get child to eat foods not preferred because they are important to child's nutrition		+
30. Child has more than one soft drink per day	+	

VI. Safety Precautions

31. Child is taught to swim or mother believes child should be taught to swim		+
32. Child is never allowed to go to a body of water unattended		+
33. Mother takes precautions in the storage of medicine		+
34. Poisonous or dangerous sprays and cleaning fluids are stored out of child's reach		+
35. Mother teaches child about danger of poisonous plants and berries in woods		+
36. Mother enforces rules about going into the streets or roads		+
37. Mother has instructed child about crossing streets or roads		+
38. Mother will never leave child alone in the house		+
39. Mother sometimes leaves child to insufficiently older sibling	+	

VII. Disease Prevention

40. Mother has encouraged child to wash hands after using toilet		+
41. Mother has encouraged child to wash hands before meals		+
42. The floors of the house appear to be swept each day		+
43. There are food scraps on the floor and furniture	+	

	Key to Scoring	
	Yes	No

VIII. Use of Medical Facilities

44. Mother has evidenced lack of awareness of child's possible dental needs — +

45. There has been neglect of fairly obvious medical needs — +

46. Mother has taken child for shots and immunizations on own initiative — — +

47. Child is taken to medical doctor or clinic after accident — — +

48. Medical care is readily sought if child is ill — — +

49. Family uses other than doctors or nurses in case of accident or illness — +

IX. Clothing

50. Child has both play clothes and good clothes — — +

51. Clothing usually appears to be hand-me-downs — +

52. Buttons and snaps of child's clothing are frequently missing and not replaced — +

53. Shoes are in reasonably good repair — — +

54. Child is usually dressed appropriately for weather conditions — — +

55. Child is usually dressed appropriately for activity — — +

56. Clothing is usually clean — — +

57. Evidence that underwear is changed as needed — — +

58. Items requiring ironing have been ironed — — +

59. Child sleeps in pajamas or gown — — +

XI. Sleeping Arrangements

60. Child has a place for sleeping at bedtime away from family living and recreation space — — +

61. Child 5 years old or older sleeps in room with parents — +

62. Some members of the family sleep more than two to a bed — +

63. At least one of the children sleeps in the same bed as parents — +

XII. Regularity of Provision for Rest

64. Bedtime for the child is set by the parents for about the same time each night — — +

76

	Key to Scoring	
	Yes	No
65. The child receives at least 9 hours of sleep most nights		+
66. The child has a routine time for arising		+

XIII. Grooming

67. There is routine washing of the child before going to bed		+
68. It is obvious that mother has given attention to child's grooming at home		+
69. Ears are usually clean		+
70. Fingernails are clean		·+
71. Head and hair is clean		+
72. Hair is combed		+
73. Hair is cut		+
74. There is a bathtub or washtub for immersed bathing in home		+
75. The child is immersed: weekly	+ (for	
never	either)	
76. Toilet tissue is usually available		+
77. Each family member has a toothbrush		+

XIV. Home Comforts

78. There is an operating electric washing machine available		+
79. Mother complains of inadequate covering for warmth	+	
80. Mattresses are in obviously poor condition	+	
81. Living room doubles as a bedroom	+	
82. Furniture is obviously in need of repair	+	
83. Home has a telephone		+
84. Family owns a car which runs		+
85. Family owns a freezer		+
86. Family owns a sewing machine		+
87. There is an operating electric sweeper		+

Items and Scoring

Part B – Emotional/Cognitive Care

		Key to Scoring	
		Yes	No
XV.	Cultural Artifacts		
88.	Family has in operating condition:		
	record player		+
	TV		+
	piano or musical instrument		+
89.	Following are available to child for play:		
	football		+
	baseball bat		+
	baseball glove		+
	play shovel		+
	dolls		+
	toys, trucks or tricycle		+
90.	There are educational toys available to the child in home		+
91.	Child owns a book of his own		+
92.	There are adult books in the house		+
93.	Newspaper is delivered regularly		+
94.	Crayons are made available to the child		+
95.	There is a dictionary in the home		+
XVI.	Parental Play with Child		
96.	Mother mentions that in past year she has:		
	Taught child something about nature		+
	Told the child a story		+
	Read a story to the child		+
97.	Mother mentions she has played games with the children		+
98.	Child is taken fishing		+
99.	Child has been taught how to use scissors		+
XVII.	Promoting Curiosity		
100.	Family has been to a town outside the county		+
101.	Planned vacation trip has been taken by the family		+
102.	Child has been taken by parents to see different animals		+
103.	Child has been taken by parents to a county fair		+
104.	Child has been taken by parents to a carnival		+

	Key to Scoring	
	Yes	No
105. Child has been taken by parents to watch construction		+
106. Child has been taken by parents to see some well-known natural attraction		+
107. Mother mentions child asks questions showing curiosity about how things work		+
108. Mother mentions that she answers child's questions about how things work		+

XVIII. Consistency in Encouraging Superego Development

109. A prayer is said before some meals		+
110. The child says prayers at bedtime		+
111. The child is spontaneously disciplined for stealing and lying		+
112. Mother mentions spontaneously that she cannot get child to mind	+	
113. Child is spontaneously punished for the use of what the mother considers profanity		+
114. Mother seems not to follow through on rewards	+	
115. Mother seems not to follow through on threatened punishments	+	
116. Mother indicates that she protects child from outside influences she considers bad: relatives or other people because of language or reputation		+

XIX. Level of Disciplinary Techniques

117. Discipline usually takes the form of: spanking with a switch	+	
very frequently no action is taken	+	
118. Child is sometimes rewarded for good behavior		+
119. Mother expresses feeling that child should cooperate without reward	+	
120. Mother threatens punishment by imagined or real fright object	+	

XX. Providing Reliable Role Image

| 121. Mother mentions that child, if son, prefers to be with father; if daughter, prefers to be with mother | | + |
| 122. Mother depends upon father for masculine tasks | | + |

	Key to Scoring	
	Yes	No
123. Mother expresses feeling that her job is the housework		+
124. Mother complains that her work is harder than father's	+	
125. Mother expresses pride in daughter's feminity or son's masculinity		+
126. Mother takes pride in her:		
Cooking		+
Sewing		+
Laundry		+
Decorating		+
Flower Garden		+
Mothering		+
Talents		+
Other		+
127. Mother mentions father's skills and hobbies:		
Hunting		+
Fishing		+
Building things with hands		+
Working on cars		+
128. Father works regularly		+
XXI. Providing Reliable Evidences of Affection		
129. Child is often ignored when he tries to tell mother something	+	
130. Mother is able to show physical affection to child comfortably		+
131. The mother taunts the child when he has had a mishap, is afraid or worried	+	
132. The mother goes to the child if he cries in the night		+
133. The child receives special attention when he is sick		+
134. The child is often pushed aside when he shows need for love	+	
135. The mother expresses to the child her concern for his safety if there is real danger	+	
136. Mother is made uncomfortable by child's demonstrations of affection	+	

Appendix B

THE MATERNAL CHARACTERISTICS SCALE

The Maternal Characteristics Scale (MCS) was designed to be used in a study observing the personalities of rural Appalachian mothers and the level of care they were providing their children. Our concern was with the mother's characteristics most closely associated with her neglectful or marginal child-caring practices. The scales were constructed to bring into focus facets of the personality that describe the Apathetic-Futile and the Impulse-Ridden mothers. Also, we included a list of characteristics associated with one's ability to express feelings verbally, which we referred to as the Composite Index of Verbal Accessibility.

The MCS assumes that the person to be rated is a female, living with her husband, and there is a child of school age in the home. Each item is a simple declarative statement that may or may not be true of the woman described. The items are concrete and objective, so that they can be answered with a simple "Yes" or "No."

Almost all statements may be answered from the worker's knowledge of and experience with the client. Although the MCS is definitely not to be self-administered or completed in the presence of the client, the caseworker may ask for specific information that she does not know, in order to fill in the form later, (e.g., "Accumulates savings" or "Belongs to a church.")

The value of the MCS to caseworkers is to sharpen their perception of personality characteristics that are helpful in making a psychodiagnosis and plan for treatment. Consequently, we do not include here a more complicated system for scoring, such as would be used in research.

We suggest that the worker use a copy of the scale (like our sample on Mrs. Smith) that does not already contain directions for scoring so that his judgment will not be influenced. After answers are indicated, the key for scoring should be referred to. The number of items on which the mother scored a minus should be subtracted from the number on which she scored a plus. The result is her final score. (She could possibly have a minus score.) If her total of plusses is one-third or more of all items pertinent, for example, to Apathy-Futility, one can assume that the mother tends toward that type of personality.

A high score on the VA Composite Index would suggest a greater degree of Verbal Accessibility, with the corresponding higher level of personality development and potential for treatment.

As an example of the scoring process and the results, we have filled in the complete MCS on Mrs. Smith, whose case was described in Chapter One. She received a score of 4 out of a total of 47 on the Apathy-Futility scale. On the Impulse-Ridden scale Mrs. Smith scored 14 out of a total of 34 items. Her Verbal Accessibility score was 7 out of 47. The research worker who saw her gave her a global VA score of 4. What does all this tell us about Mrs. Smith? First, we already knew that she is immature. Now we know that she is more impulsive than she is apathetic and futile, and although she is not completely inaccessible, there will be some difficulty in getting her to express feelings in a casework relationship.

Again we emphasize that the value for the worker of the MCS lies primarily in bringing to his attention a number of observable characteristics that will help him evaluate the mother's personality.

THE MATERNAL CHARACTERISTICS SCALE
The Apathy-Futility Scale

Sequence Numbering	Item	Direction for Scoring	
		Yes	No
1.	Claims that she is unable to perform at job or housework or get anything done.	+	
2.	Speaks of herself as healthy, strong and energetic.	–	
3.	Face is sometimes dirty, or makeup is smeared despite availability of washing facilities.	+	
4.	Hair is usually unkempt, tangled or matted.	+	
5.	Clothes are usually dirty or in disarray.	+	
6.	Clothing is appropriate to the season.	–	
7.	Clothing is appropriate to the occasion.	–	
8.	Usually stands or sits erect, with concern for posture.	–	
9.	Speech is full of long pauses.	+	
10.	Daydreams much of the time; gets out of touch with current daily happenings.	+	
11.	From time to time becomes preoccupied or shows lapses of attention during conversation.	+	
12.	Speaks in a faint voice, or voice fades away at end of sentences.	+	
13.	Talks comfortably with interviewer by second contact.	–	
14.	In discussing children, frequently adverts to self.	+	
15.	Talks in ambiguous, obscure, vague or cryptic manner.	+	
16.	Shows warmth in tone in discussing her children.	–	
17.	Shows warmth in tone when talking with her children.	–	
18.	Answers questions with single words or phrases only.	+	
19.	Sometimes expresses hostility through physical aggression.	–	
20.	Has a sad expression or holds her body in a dejected or despondent posture.	+	
21.	Shows warmth in gestures with interviewer.	–	

Sequence Numbering	Item	Direction for Scoring	
		Yes	No
22.	Evidences fearfulness or shyness about meeting new people or strange social situation.	+	
23.	When frustrated, flies into rages.		–
24.	Shows enthusiasm.		–
25.	Is usually agressive.		–
26.	When frustrated, creates a turmoil.		–
27.	Visits with neighbors.		–
28.	Seems incurious about the inner feelings of others.	+	
29.	Has at one time shown capacity to hold a job.		–
30.	Expects companionship from husband.		–
31.	Appears indifferent to husband's behavior.	+	
32.	Appears surprisingly accepting of husband's irresponsible behavior.	+	
33.	Shares problems with husband.		–
34.	Clings to husband in fearful, dependent way.	+	
35.	Visits with husband's family.		–
36.	Shares family decision making with husband.		–
37.	Discusses her children freely.		–
38.	Individualizes her children noticeably.		–
39.	Discusses her children's behavior as if "from the outside."	+	
40.	Manages family finances.		–
41.	Belongs to PTA.		–
42.	Belongs to church.		–
43.	Belongs to other community group.		–
44.	Keeps virtually the same posture throughout the interview.	+	
45.	Keeps eyes closed or averted.	+	
46.	Has decorated house in some unexpected way.		–
47.	Shows interest in and knowledge of larger world scene.		–

The Impulsivity Scale

Sequence Numbering	Item	Direction for Scoring Yes	No
1.	Lacks persistence in pursuit of goals.	+	
2.	Plans realistically for herself, children, family.	–	
3.	Follows through on plans that have been made for herself, children, family.	–	
4.	Has definite, realistic goals for self, children, family.	–	
5.	Shouts, yells or screams frequently at something or somebody in interviewer's presence.	+	
6.	Whines when she talks.	+	
7.	Dwells on her problems with her children.	+	
8.	Sometimes expresses hostility through physical aggression.	+	
9.	Evidences gullibility.	+	
10.	Has shown defiance toward authorities in word and deed.	+	
11.	When frustrated, flies into rages.	+	
12.	When frustrated, creates a turmoil.	+	
13.	Shows tolerance of routine.	–	
14.	Clings to her husband in fearful, dependent way.	+	
15.	Leaves most family decisions to her husband.	+	
16.	Apparently married to escape an unpleasant home situation.	+	
17.	Takes pleasure in things she and children do together.	+	
18.	Clings to her children.	+	
19.	Sets and maintains control on her own behavior.		+
20.	Has engaged in behavior not acceptable in her community.	+	
21.	Can make decisions and take responsibility for them.	–	
22.	Has at one time shown capacity to hold a job.	–	
23.	Complains of feeling neglected by her parents.	+	
24.	Seems to treat all adults as if they were parents.	+	
25.	Frequently refers to opinions of, or quotes her mother.	+	

Sequence Numbering	Item	Direction for Scoring Yes	No
26.	Frequently refers to opinions of, or quotes her father.	+	
27.	Accumulates savings.	–	
28.	Visits with her own family only.	+	
29.	Expresses warmth in exaggerated form.	+	
30.	Often buys things impulsively.	+	
31.	Talks of ambitions for self or family which, though not impossible, are extremely unlikely.	+	
32.	Takes pleasure in her children's adventures.	+	
33.	Shows belligerence toward interviewer from time to time.	+	
34.	Keeps insisting that interviewer give advice or intervene on her behalf.	+	

Verbal Accessibility Scale

Sequence Numbering	Item	Direction for Scoring Yes	No
1.	Evidences (some verbalization) negative or discouraged attitude toward future accomplishments or attainments.	+	
2.	Mentions she is aimless or getting nowhere.	+	
3.	Says she enjoys living.	+	
4.	Evidences excessive concern with religion or expresses some highly unusual religious ideas.	+	
5.	Claims she is unable to perform at job or house work or get anything done.	+	
6.	Speaks of herself as healthy, strong, energetic.	+	
7.	It is hard for her to consider a new way of looking at same thing.	–	
8.	From time to time becomes preoccupied or shows lapses of attention.		+
9.	Speech is full of long pauses.	–	
10.	Speaks in a faint voice or voice fades away at end of sentences.	–	
11.	Talks comfortably with interviewer by the second contact.	+	
12.	Usually states opinions reasonably directly.	+	

The Maternal Characteristics Scale

Sequence Numbering	Item	Direction for Scoring Yes	No
13.	Talks in an ambiguous, obscure, vague or cryptic manner.	−	
14.	Whines when she talks.	−	
15.	Feels free to verbalize regarding hurts received.	+	
16.	Expresses ideas of revenge and wishes to retaliate.	+	
17.	Evidences a sense of humor.	+	
18.	Verbalizes embarrassment.	+	
19.	Verbalizes shame.	+	
20.	Verbalizes guilt.	+	
21.	Enjoys talking about herself.	+	
22.	Answers questions with single words or by phrases only.	−	
23.	Talks of her situation with practically no outward sign of emotion.	−	
24.	Shows warmth in voice much of time with interviewer.	+	
25.	Shows warmth in tone in discussing her children.	+	
26.	Shows warmth in tone in talking with her children.	+	
27.	Can laugh at herself.	+	
28.	Expresses boredom with her life.	+	
29.	Shares problems with her husband.	+	
30.	Shares plans with her husband.	+	
31.	Shares plans for children with her husband.	+	
32.	Shares conversation with her husband.	+	
33.	Is able to say she enjoys sex.	+	
34.	Shares family decision making with husband.	+	
35.	Discusses her children freely.	+	
36.	Individualizes her children noticeably.	+	
37.	Discusses her children's behavior as if from the outside.	−	
38.	Discusses her children's assets.	+	
39.	Discusses her children's liabilities.	+	
40.	Speaks with pride of personal achievement or possession.	+	
41.	Complains of feeling neglected by parents.	+	
42.	Keeps eyes closed or averted.	−	

Sequence Numbering	Item	Direction for Scoring	
		Yes	No
43.	Expresses objection to interview or resentment at having to answer questions.		
44.	Expresses awareness of complexities in others' decisions; that they have to weigh alternatives.	+	
45.	Manner of response or failure to respond makes it uncertain whether or not many items are true (e.g., subject incoherent, evasive, suggestible).	−	
46.	Frequently, and appropriately, expresses herself in abstractions.	+	
47.	Uses figures or speech colorfully or amusingly.	+	

NOTE: This VA scale from the MCS is scored so that a high + score means high Verbal Accessibility. In this way the high score is different in meaning from those on the other two scales, which are scored in the pathological direction.

THE MATERNAL CHARACTERISTICS SCALE
Sample Forms for Mrs. Smith
The Apathy-Futility Scale

Sequence Numbering	Item	Scoring Yes	Scoring No
1.	Claims that she is unable to perform at job or housework or get anything done.		+
2.	Speaks of herself as healthy, strong and energetic.		+
3.	Face is sometimes dirty, or makeup is smeared despite availability of washing facilities.	+	
4.	Hair is usually unkempt, tangled or matted.	+	
5.	Clothes are usually dirty or in disarray.	+	
6.	Clothing is appropriate to the season.	+	
7.	Clothing is appropriate to the occasion.	+	
8.	Usually stands or sits erect, with concern for posture.		+
9.	Speech is full of long pauses.		+
10.	Daydreams much of the time; gets out of touch with current daily happenings.		+
11.	From time to time becomes preoccupied or shows lapses of attention during conversation.	+	
12.	Speaks in a faint voice, or voice fades away at end of sentences.		+
13.	Talks comfortably with interviewer by second contact.		+
14.	In discussing children, frequently adverts to self.	+	
15.	Talks in ambiguous, obscure, vague, or cryptic manner.	+	
16.	Shows warmth in tone in discussing her children.	+	
17.	Shows warmth in tone when talking with her children.	+	
18.	Answers questions with single words or phrases only.	+	
19.	Sometimes expresses hostility through physical aggression.		+
20.	Has a sad expression or holds her body in a dejected or despondent posture.	+	
21.	Shows warmth in gestures with interviewer.		+
22.	Evidences fearfulness or shyness about meeting new people or strange social situation.	+	
23.	When frustrated, flies into rages.		+

89

Sequence Numbering	Item	Scoring Yes	No
24.	Shows enthusiasm.		+
25.	Is usually aggressive.		+
26.	When frustrated, creates a turmoil.		+
27.	Visits with neighbors.		+
28.	Seems incurious about the inner feelings of others.	+	
29.	Has at one time shown capacity to hold a job.		+
30.	Expects companionship from husband.	+	
31.	Appears indifferent to husband's behavior.	+	
32.	Appears surprisingly accepting of husband's irresponsible behavior.	+	
33.	Shares problems with husband.	+	
34.	Clings to husband in fearful, dependent way.	+	
35.	Visits with husband's family.	+	
36.	Shares family decision making with husband.	+	
37.	Discusses her children freely.	+	
38.	Individualizes children noticeably.	+	
39.	Discusses her children's behavior as if "from the outside."		+
40.	Manages family finances.		+
41.	Belongs to PTA.		+
42.	Belongs to church.		+
43.	Belongs to other community group.		+
44.	Keeps virtually the same posture throughout the interview.	+	
45.	Keeps eyes closed or averted.		+
46.	Has decorated house in some unexpected way.		+
47.	Shows interest in and knowledge of larger world scene.		+

Scoring

Total number plus items - - - - - - - - - - - - - - - 14
Total number minus items - - - - - - - - - - - - - - 10
Mrs. Smith's Apathy-Futility Score - - - - - - - +4

Sample Forms for Mrs. Smith

The Impulsivity Scale

Number	Item	Yes	No
1.	Lacks persistence in pursuit of goals.	+	
2.	Plans realistically for herself, children, family.		+

The Maternal Characteristics Scale

Number	Item	Yes	No
3.	Follows through on plans that have been made for herself, children, family.		+
4.	Has definite, realistic goals for self, children, family.		+
5.	Shouts, yells or screams frequently at something or somebody in interviewer's presence.	+	
6.	Whines when she talks.	+	
7.	Dwells on her problems with her children.	+	
8.	Sometimes expresses hostility through physical aggression.		+
9.	Evidences gullibility.	+	
10.	Has shown defiance toward authorities in word and deed.		+
11.	When frustrated, flies into rages.		+
12.	When frustrated, creates a turmoil.		+
13.	Shows tolerance of routine.	+	
14.	Clings to her husband in fearful, dependent way.	+	
15.	Leaves most family decisions to her husband.	+	
16.	Apparently married to escape an unpleasant home situation.	+	
17.	Takes pleasure in things she and children do together.		+
18.	Clings to her children.	+	
19.	Sets and maintains control on her own behavior.	+	
20.	Has engaged in behavior not acceptable in her community.		+
21.	Can make decisions and take responsibility for them.		+
22.	Has at one time shown capacity to hold a job.		+
23.	Complains of feeling neglected by her parents.		+
24.	Seems to treat all adults as if they were parents.	+	
25.	Frequently refers to opinions of, or quotes her mother.	+	
26.	Frequently refers to opinions of, or quotes her father.		+
27.	Accumulates savings.		+
28.	Visits with her own family only.		+
29.	Expresses warmth in exaggerated form.		+
30.	Often buys things impulsively.	+	
31.	Talks of ambitions for self or family which, though not impossible, are extremely unlikely.	+	

Number	Item	Yes	No
32.	Takes pleasure in her children's adventures.		+
33.	Shows belligerence toward interviewer from time to time.	+	
34.	Keeps insisting that interviewer give advice or intervene on her behalf.	+	

Scoring

Total number plus items - - - - - - - - - - - - - - 15
Total number minus items - - - - - - - - - - - - - 1
Mrs. Smith's Impulsivity Score - - - - - - - - - - +14

Sample Forms for Mrs. Smith

Verbal-Accessibility Scale

Number	Item	Yes	No
1.	Evidences (some verbalization) negative or discouraged attitude toward future accomplishments or attainments.		+
2.	Mentions she is aimless or getting nowhere.		+
3.	Says she enjoys living.	+	
4.	Evidences excessive concern with religion or expresses some highly unusual religious ideas.		+
5.	Claims she is unable to perform at job or housework or get anything done.		+
6.	Speaks of herself as healthy, strong, energetic.		+
7.	It is hard for her to consider a new way of looking at the same thing.	+	
8.	From time to time becomes preoccupied or shows lapses of attention.	+	
9.	Speech is full of long pauses.		+
10.	Speaks in a faint voice or voice fades away at end of sentences.		+
11.	Talks comfortably with interviewer by the second contact.		+
12.	Usually states opinions reasonably directly.		+
13.	Talks in an ambiguous, obscure, vague or cryptic manner.	+	
14.	Whines when she talks.	+	
15.	Feels free to verbalize regarding hurts received.		+
16.	Expresses ideas of revenge and wishes to retaliate.		+
17.	Evidences a sense of humor.		+
18.	Verbalizes embarrassment.		+

The Maternal Characteristics Scale

Number	Item	Yes	No
19.	Verbalizes shame.		+
20.	Verbalizes guilt.		+
21.	Enjoys talking about herself.	+	
22.	Answers questions with single words or phrases only.	+	
23.	Talks of her situation with practically no outward sign of emotion.	+	
24.	Shows warmth in voice much of time with interviewer.		+
25.	Shows warmth in tone in discussing her children.	+	
26.	Shows warmth in tone in talking with her children.	+	
27.	Can laugh at herself.		+
28.	Expresses boredom with her life.		+
29.	Shares problems with her husband.	+	
30.	Shares plans with her husband.	+	
31.	Shares plans for children with her husband.	+	
32.	Shares conversation with her husband.	+	
33.	Is able to say she enjoys sex.		+
34.	Shares family decision making with husband.	+	
35.	Discusses her children freely.	+	
36.	Individualizes her children noticeably.	+	
37.	Discusses her children's behavior as if "from the outside."	+	
38.	Discusses her children's assets.	+	
39.	Discusses her children's liabilities.	+	
40.	Speaks with pride of personal achievement or possession.	+	
41.	Complains of feeling neglected by parents.		+
42.	Keeps eyes closed or averted.		+
43.	Expresses objection to interview or resentment at having to answer questions.	+	
44.	Expresses awareness of complexities in others' decisions; that they have to weigh alternatives.		+
45.	Manner of response or failure to respond makes it uncertain whether or not many of the items are true (e.g., subject incoherent, evasive, suggestible).		+
46.	Frequently, and appropriately, expresses herself in abstractions.		+
47.	Uses figures of speech colorfully or amusingly.		+

Scoring

Total number plus items - - - - - - - - - - - - - - 14

Total number minus items - - - - - - - - - - - - - 7

Mrs. Smith's Verbal-Accessibility Score - - - - +7

NOTE: This VA scale is scored so that a high + score means high VA. In this way the high score is different in meaning from those on the other two scales, which are scored in the pathological direction.